DEPARTMENT OF INTERNATIONAL ECONOMIC AND SOCIAL AFFAIRS
Centre for Social Development and Humanitarian Affairs

migrant workers

No. 2

THE SOCIAL SITUATION
OF MIGRANT WORKERS AND THEIR FAMILIES

UNITED NATIONS
New York, 1986

NOTE

ST/ESA/189

UNITED NATIONS PUBLICATION
Sales No. E.86.IV.11
ISBN 92-1-130118-1
01100P

This publication is No. 2 in a series on migrant workers. The first publication in the series is entitled *Pertinent Legislative and Administrative Regulations on the Welfare of Migrant Workers and their Families* (Sales No. E.83.IV.2).

CONTENTS

	Page
Abbreviations	2
INTRODUCTION	3

Chapter

I. RECENT TRENDS IN THE INTERNATIONAL MIGRATION OF WORKERS ... 5

  A. Western Europe ... 5

  B. Middle East and North Africa ... 8

  C. South and North America ... 12

  D. Africa ... 12

  E. Asia ... 15

  F. Conclusion ... 16

II. MAJOR EMERGING PROBLEMS CONCERNING THE WELFARE OF MIGRANT WORKERS AND THEIR FAMILIES AND MEASURES TO SOLVE THOSE PROBLEMS ... 18

  A. Legal insecurity ... 18

  B. The protection of the family ... 19

  C. Adaptation to and integration into the country of employment ... 31

  D. Return to and reintegration into the country of origin ... 47

III. CONCLUDING REMARKS ... 55

Tables

1. Young aliens under 25 years of age in certain countries of employment ... 7

2. Labour migrants to the Middle East from selected Asian countries, 1975-1983 ... 10

3. South American region: estimated number of migrant workers in 1974 ... 13

4. Employment of foreign Africans by country of origin, 1975-1981 ... 14

Abbreviations

API	Arab Planning Institute
ASEAN	Association of South-East Asian Nations
EEC	European Economic Community
ESCWA	Economic and Social Commission for Western Asia
ILO	International Labour Organisation
OECD	Organisation for Economic Co-operation and Development
UNESCO	United Nations Educational, Scientific and Cultural Organization
UNDP	United Nations Development Programme

INTRODUCTION

The Economic and Social Council, in its resolution 1983/16 of 26 May 1983, requested the Secretary-General to prepare, in co-operation with the specialized agencies and other organizations concerned, a report on the situation of migrant workers and their families in which the needs and problems emerging as a result of the changing conditions of international migration would be fully taken into account, and to submit that report to the Commission for Social Development at its twenty-ninth session.

In compliance with this request, the Centre for Social Development and Humanitarian Affairs of the Department of International Economic and Social Affairs undertook a study on the contemporary situation of migrant workers and their families, with special reference to their social needs and problems resulting from certain significant developments, brought about by the economic crisis, in the conditions of international migration of labour over the past ten years. The major findings of the study were incorporated in the report of the Secretary-General to the twenty-ninth session of the Commission for Social Development (E/CN.5/1985/8).

In the report, recent trends in the international migration of workers were analysed; the problems confronting migrants in the most important areas of their social life, such as the protection of families, adaptation to and integration in the host country, return to and reintegration into the country of origin, were examined; and the ways in which these problems might be solved and the adequacy of existing social programmes were considered.

In assessing the present pattern of international labour migration, the study focused on the social consequences of two major developments: the new situation of intra-European migration and a profound change in the nature and scale of international labour migration in the Middle East. In Western Europe, the new situation was created as a result of the closing of the door to large-scale migration of foreign manpower in 1973-1974, coupled with the shift of emphasis to repatriation of migrant workers and their families to their countries of origin, on the one hand, and the continuation of migration to Western Europe of dependants admitted for family reunification purposes, on the other hand. This has led to a radical change in the composition of the foreign population in Europe and, consequently, to the emergence of some serious problems of social integration among migrants.

Owing to a dramatic increase in inflows of temporary workers to the petroleum-producing countries of the Middle East from different parts of the world, but mainly from Asian countries, a number of serious social issues have emerged. Major labour-importing States of the region appear not to be moving toward social integration of their large foreign population; they severely restrict family migration and make little effort to extend to migrants economic and social benefits, let alone political rights.

The present study has been prepared on the basis of recent reports prepared by the United Nations on the welfare of migrant workers and their families, information received from the international organizations concerned, particularly the International Labour Organisation (ILO), the United Nations Educational, Scientific and Cultural Organization (UNESCO), the Council of Europe and the Organisation for Economic Co-operation and Development (OECD), as well as national data, which was made available for the Secretary-General by Member States, in accordance with resolution 1981/21 of 6 May 1981 of the Economic and Social Council. In addition, six consultants (Fred Arnold (Hawaii), Emil Hersak (Yugoslavia), Donald K. Kowet (Sweden), Silvia Lépore

(Argentina), Bassem Sirhan (Kuwait) and Melita Svob (Yugoslavia)) were appointed in order to obtain an overview of the social situation of migrant workers and their families in Africa, Asia, Europe, Latin America and the Middle East.

I. RECENT TRENDS IN THE INTERNATIONAL MIGRATION OF WORKERS

The migration of workers from one country to another has become one of the central characteristic features of the global economic system. Although estimating how many people leave their own country to look for work is very difficult, by a rough count there are about 20 million workers employed outside their own countries, with an unknown number of dependants. 1/ International migration for employment and better income-earning opportunities has taken place in most regions of the world. A large number of people are involved in movements among the developing countries themselves. Movements from one developed market economy country to another are quite substantial in some instances. Most numerous, however, are migrations from developing countries to developed market economy countries. About 12 million migrants from the developing world are estimated to be working in the developed market economy countries and in the high-income petroleum-exporting countries of the Middle East. 2/ Compared with the general picture of migratory movements in the world, described in the report of the Secretary-General to the Commission for Social Development in 1975 (E/CN.5/515), the present pattern of international labour migration is distinguished by at least two important factors: (a) the new situation of intra-European migration, brought about by the economic crisis; and (b) a profound change in the nature and scale of international labour migration in the Middle East.

A. Western Europe

In Western Europe, the economic crisis has resulted in the drastic curtailment of numbers of migrant workers, especially in the countries that have attracted the largest migration streams, such as France, the Federal Republic of Germany and Switzerland. In these countries, after 1974, the virtual stoppage of traditional labour immigration has been accompanied by administrative measures to encourage migrants to return home. It is estimated that since 1974, this inversion of the migratory flow has affected more than 1.5 million workers. 3/ This development creates considerable difficulties for the traditional labour-exporting countries. Being weaker and less developed than the major receiving countries, the sending countries have to face the same economic crisis and, in addition, have to contend with the drastic reduction, or even cessation, of employment abroad, the influx of returning migrants into a frequently over-burdened labour market and the decreasing flow of foreign currency earnings in the form of workers' remittances.

The employment of foreign migrant workers in Western Europe reached its highest level of about 6 million in the early 1970s. 4/ An OECD report reveals that about 5,221,600 migrant workers held jobs at that time, and were accompanied by almost as many dependants. The largest importer of labour was the Federal Republic of Germany (2,081,900), followed by France (1,591,900), Switzerland (515,100), Belgium (332,200), Sweden (233,500), Austria (176,300) and Luxembourg (52,200). Among the major labour-exporting countries were Italy (818,800), Turkey (772,700), Yugoslavia (541,100), Portugal (528,700), Algeria (385,500) and Spain (324,100).

Since 1973/74, certain traditional flows of workers have been very much reduced. However, the interruption in the recruitment of new foreign workers has not meant a complete stoppage in the flow of workers. In addition, since re-immigration became impossible, many migrants decided to stay in the receiving countries longer and brought their families there. As a result, foreign populations declined only in Switzerland. In other receiving countries, the number of foreigners has actually increased. 5/ According to

recent data of the Council of Europe, the foreign populations resident in the
territories of member States are continuing to grow. The Council estimates
that a total of between 14 and 15 million persons have settled outside their
own countries of origin. Foreign workers made up a significant proportion of
the labour force in 1982, ranging from 34.4 per cent in Luxembourg to 17 per
cent in Switzerland, 7.8 per cent in the Federal Republic of Germany, 7.7 per
cent in Belgium, 7.1 per cent in France, 5.8 per cent in Austria, 5.3 per cent
in Sweden and 4.3 per cent in the Netherlands. 6/

The growth of the foreign population is being accompanied by a radical
transformation of its components, as a result of two major trends: an
increase in the female component, and the addition of children born in the
host countries or admitted to join their families.

As early as 1971, the number of foreign men working in Austria, Belgium
and Switzerland was 20 per cent higher than the number of women, while the
ratio of men to women was 150-160 to 100 in France and the Federal Republic of
Germany. Since 1973, the proportion of women among immigrants has grown
considerably in all European receiving countries. According to an OECD
estimate, this proportion was between 40 and 46 per cent during the period
1975/80: Austria (1980) 40 per cent, Belgium (1977) 46.9 per cent, France
(1975) 40.1 per cent, Federal Republic of Germany (1980) 43.6 per cent, the
Netherlands (1980) 41.7 per cent, Sweden (1978) 48.3 per cent and Switzerland
(1980) 45.9 per cent. In five major European immigration countries (Belgium,
France, the Federal Republic of Germany, Sweden, Switzerland), the number of
female immigrants was put at over 4 million by the end of the 1970s. In most
countries, this steeply upward trend was more or less uniform, from about 30
per cent in the 1960s to some 45 per cent in the 1980s, and has been observed
for all nationalities. The considerable growth of the immigrant female
population over the last few years is still continuing, and in the medium and
long term, women may make up the largest part of the population of foreign
origin.

The substantial participation of immigrant women in the labour force is a
factor common to all European countries. Immigrant women are characterized by
high participation rates, higher on average than those of local women. Average
rates reflect considerable differences between nationalities, for some of whom
they are extremely high: for example, in Sweden in 1980, the participation
rates for Finnish, Yugoslav and Greek women were 78 per cent, 84 per cent and
86 per cent respectively. 7/

Another interesting recent development in terms of the composition of
foreign populations in Europe is the growing proportion of the youngest age
groups. The importance of the current phenomenon can be seen from table 1
below. In nine principal receiving countries (excluding Austria and Italy),
there are nearly 4.7 million young people under 25 years of age who officially
possess a foreign nationality.

It appears from this table that: (a) in all countries except Switzerland
the proportion of young people aged between 0 and 24 years in the foreign
population is between 40 per cent (France, Germany, the Federal Republic of,
Luxembourg, Norway, Sweden) and 50 per cent (Belgium, the Netherlands), while
Denmark occupies an intermediate position (43.3 per cent); (b) in all
countries, the proportion of young people under 25 years of age is higher
among foreigners than among nationals. The greatest differences noted were in
Belgium, the Netherlands, Luxembourg and then Denmark and Sweden (15, 12, 10
and 8 percentage points respectively).

Table 1. Young aliens under 25 years of age in
certain countries of employment
(Numbers and percentages)

Country	Numbers (both sexes)	Percentage of young aliens to total aliens	Percentage of young nationals to total nationals
Belgium	438 000	50.0	34.8
Denmark	44 000	43.3	35.1
France	1 478 000	41.5	38.0
Germany, Federal Republic of	1 855 000	40.1	33.1
Luxembourg	39 000	42.7	32.1
Netherlands	273 000	50.8	38.2
Norway	34 000	39.6	36.8
Sweden	163 000	40.2	32.1
Switzerland	335 500	36.9	34.2

Source: Council of Europe, "Report on the situation of migrant workers and members of their families", Second Conference of European Ministers Responsible for Migration Affairs, Strasbourg, 1983, p. 6.

To assess the current situation of the migrant population in Europe, several important factors have to be taken into account.

First, according to all available data, the number of returnees to the country of origin tend to decline or to remain at a relatively low level. In 1974 and 1975, a period immediately following the onset of the economic crisis, an acceleration in the number of departures from the countries of employment was observed, whereas from 1976 to 1981 the numbers declined steadily.

Secondly, owing to the low rate of returning migrants on the one hand, and the continuing reunion of families on the other, the external migration balances of major receiving countries are positive.

Thirdly, the closing of frontiers to new migrant workers by the major receiving countries has led to a stabilization of the foreign population in these countries. As a result, the period of residence of migrants in the country of employment is growing longer in all receiving countries. In the Federal Republic of Germany, in 1981, for example, the average duration of residence was nine and a half years. In France, in 1981, 70 per cent of the foreigners had been resident for more than 11 years. In Switzerland, in 1982, 80 per cent of immigrants had been resident for six years or more.

All the above-mentioned developments in the international migration of labour in Europe will undoubtedly broaden the composition of the labour force as well as of the host societies at large.

It is also important to note an increase in illegal migration to Western Europe. The phenomenon is largely a consequence of the blocking of the official channels of immigration combined with the continued existence of possibilities for the employment of foreigners. An easy crossing of State borders with a tourist visa has only stimulated the development of this trend in recent years. On the one hand, however, "illegal" migration has always been in the shadow of other, regular, migration flows, as a hasty solution to the problem of administrative hindrances. Information channels, which have normally affected the intensification of migration from a certain country, have also affected an increase in illegal migration, especially after the period from 1973 to 1974.

Most Governments in Western Europe have adopted measures of tighter control, but these do not seem to be successful in stemming the continuing flow of illegal migrants. At present, strict policies to deal with undocumented migration are applied in a majority of States members of the European Economic Community (EEC). There has been a growing tendency to impose stricter penalties on the employers of illegal migrants, although most continue to impose penalties on the workers themselves. France, for example, expelled some 25,000 illegal migrants in 1978 and an additional 28,000 in 1979. In 1981, the Government proclaimed a policy of "humanizing and controlling" illegal migration, announcing that it intended to regularize the status of migrants who were in stable employment. The regularization process was expected to involve as many as 300,000 illegal migrants.

B. Middle East and North Africa

The international migration of labour is of crucial significance in the Arab world. The volume of migration for employment in the region increased significantly after 1973 in response to the large-scale development plans that have been implemented by the oil-producing States, in particular Kuwait, the Libyan Arab Jamahiriya, Qatar, Saudi Arabia and the United Arab Emirates. In 1980, according to a recent ILO estimate, 8/ there were around 2,822,000 migrant workers in the oil-exporting countries of the Middle East and North Africa. Of these, 1,023,250 were in Saudi Arabia, 545,500 in the Libyan Arab Jamahiriya, 411,000 in the United Arab Emirates, 378,700 in Kuwait, 96,800 in Oman, and 125,500 in Iraq. Among the major labour-supplying countries were Egypt (695,650), Pakistan (371,630), Yemen (336,145), India (280,450), Jordan (250,350) other Asian countries (168,500). Because of an increasing demand for foreign labour in the capital-rich countries of the region, the volume of the migrant population is constantly growing and, according to the latest World Bank projections, will increase at a considerable rate in the near future. It was predicted that in 1985 migrant communities would account for 4.3 million migrant workers and 6.6 million dependants. This might be a low estimate, however.

One of the most salient features of recent migratory trends in the region is the dramatic increase in the number of Asian workers employed by the oil-exporting countries in the Middle East. Because of the relative recency of Asian labour migration to the Middle East, accurate statistical systems to measure the flow of workers have not yet been fully developed. The labour-importing countries in the Middle East have been reluctant to release information on their foreign work-forces and the statistics available from the major sending countries in Asia are often incomplete and inaccurate. Nevertheless, a careful examination of the estimates available permits the general order of magnitude to be established.

Table 2 shows the annual outflow of Asian workers to the Middle East between 1975 and 1983. The last (tenth) row of figures in the table indicates the best available estimates of the stock of Asian workers in the Middle East. In 1981, there were nearly 2.5 million Asian migrant workers in the Middle East (not including accompanying dependants). 9/ Most of the workers came from India and Pakistan, but a substantial number of them also came from Bangladesh, the Philippines, the Republic of Korea and Thailand. The number of Asian workers leaving for the Middle East each year has soared since the 1973 oil embargo and the subsequent rapid expansion in the economic and social development plans of the oil-exporting countries in the Middle East. In 1983, alone, it is estimated that about 1 million Asian workers left for the Middle East. These estimates are considerably higher than earlier projections, which did not take full account of the increasing share of Asian workers among all foreign workers in the Middle East.

In the last two or three years, there has been a great deal of discussion about substantially reducing the number of foreign workers in several Middle Eastern countries. The decrease in the price of oil has forced these countries to postpone some major construction projects and to cancel others. The continuing decline in the financial reserves of the oil exporters has also been a cause for concern. Moreover, political tensions and security concerns in the Middle East have added further to the uncertainty. Nevertheless, there is, as yet, no evidence of a substantial cut-back in the overall demand for Asian workers and few Asians have been sent home before the end of their contracts.

The vast majority of the workers from East and South-East Asia go to a single country: Saudi Arabia (86 per cent of land-based workers from the Philippines, 68 per cent of workers from the Republic of Korea, and 85 per cent of recent labour migrants from Thailand). Workers from South Asia, however, are more evenly spread throughout the region. About half of the migrants from Pakistan are working in Saudi Arabia, but only about one quarter of the migrants from Bangladesh, India and Sri Lanka are working in Saudi Arabia. Other major receiving countries include Bahrain, Iraq, Kuwait, the Libyan Arab Jamahiriya, Oman, Qatar and the United Arab Emirates.

The crucial importance of migrant labour in receiving countries of the region can be proved by the fact that in several of these countries, foreign workers outnumber the nationals by large margins. Their share in total employment is about 90 per cent in the United Arab Emirates, 77 per cent in Qatar, 71 per cent in Kuwait and 64 per cent in Oman. 10/

Migrant workers are found in every occupation and in every economic sector. The largest group of migrants work in construction, followed by personal and household services, followed by manufacturing industries, then by trade and restaurants and then by transport, storage and communications. A relatively smaller number of migrants work in economic sectors, such as agriculture, fishing and hunting, mining and quarrying and financial institutions, since these sectors can employ only a small nubmer of workers. The majority of migrants are unskilled workers and manual labourers working in building and construction, household services and manufacturing industries. The rest of migrant labour is distributed among clerical jobs, semi-skilled and skilled occupations, administrative and professional occupations.

Table 2. Labour migrants to the Middle East from selected Asian Countries, 1975-1983 a/

Year	Labour migrants to the Middle East					All foreign labour migrants	
	India	Philippines	Sri Lanka	Thailand	Bangladesh	Pakistan	Philippines
1975	..	1 552	..	984	..	23 077	12 501
1976	4 200	7 812	526	1 287	6 087	41 690	19 221
1977	22 900	25 721	633	3 870	15 725	140 522	36 676
1978	69 000	34 441	8 082	14 215	22 809	130 525	50 961
1979	171 000	73 210	20 980	8 329	24 485	125 507	92 519
1980	236 200	132 044	24 053	20 475	30 573	129 847	157 394
1981	276 000	183 582	47 800	23 848	55 787	168 403	210 936
1982	239 545	210 972	..	105 143	62 805	142 945	314 284
1983 (January-June)	(119 000)	(161 699) b/	..	(40 199)	(32 920)	..	..
Stock (1981)	800 000	342 300	50 000	159 000	178 500	800 200	..

Source: Fred Arnold and Nasra M. Shah, "Asian labor migration to the Middle-East", International Migration Review, vol. XVIII, No. 2, pp. 294-317.

a/ All estimates are for workers to the Middle East only except for Bangladesh and Pakistan, which include all foreign labour migrants. The 1981 stock estimate for Pakistan is based on workers in the Middle East only. The estimates do not include dependents who accompany labour migrants to the Middle East.

b/ This is one half of the estimate of 323,398 for all of 1983.

Data available on the characteristics of Asian migrant workers in the Middle East reveal that the majority of them are young married males, predominantly of rural origin. Nearly all migrant workers from India and Bangladesh are male. The Philippines is the only country that sends a substantial number of women to the Middle East. For example, more than half of all the Filipino professional and technical workers in the Middle East are women (56 per cent) as are more than one third of the service workers. 11/ However, almost none of the Filipino production or construction workers in the Middle East are female.

The lack of female migrant workers in the Middle East is related to both the supply of women who want to work there and the demand for female workers by the labour-importing countries. Jobs for women in the Middle East are scarce and many Asian women are reluctant to work there because of cultural differences and difficult working conditions. Several Asian countries have also placed restrictions on the emigration of women for contract work. For example, Pakistani women under 45 years of age are barred from accepting employment as maids in the Middle East by the Emigration Ordinance of 1979, 12/ and the Ministry of the Interior in Thailand has a policy of not allowing women to work in some Middle East countries because of differences in customs and culture, which may result in hardship or trouble. 13/

With the exception of the Special Survey in India, conducted around 1977-1978, every study in Asia has reported that about two thirds or more of all migrant workers are married. The average migrant worker in the Middle East supports four to six dependants in the sending country. As mentioned earlier, few of these workers take their families with them to their country of employment.

The majority of Asian migrant workers in the Middle East are production/ transport workers (including construction workers). Substantial numbers of migrant workers are also employed as service workers and professional/technical workers. Only a minority are unskilled labourers. In the future, as the pace of construction slows, it is expected that the demand for foreign workers will increasingly shift away from construction towards such areas as maintenance and services.

The consequences of Asian labour migration for the worker, the worker's family, and the sending communities depend in large measure on the length of time the worker is employed abroad. Most contracts for Asian workers in the Middle East run for one or two years (one-year contracts are most common), although contracts for professionals are sometimes longer. Despite the short length of most contracts, extensions may be granted, contracts may be renewed and workers may return on entirely new contracts after they have gone home. Thus, the average length of stay for Asian migrant workers in the Middle East exceeds the average contract length by a substantial margin. For example, the average Filipino migrant worker has been employed overseas for three years 14/ and returning Pakistani overseas worker have spent an average of five years abroad. 15/ Most workers, however, are able to take advantage of the opportunity for annual home leave, and this somewhat lessens the impact of lengthy absences.

Information on the number of dependants living with Asian migrant workers in the Middle East is quite sketchy. It is clear, however, that the vast majority of Asian migrant workers in the Middle East leave their families behind. It has been estimated that only 4 per cent of Pakistani workers in the Middle East are accompanied by their families, leaving approximately 3 million women and children in Pakistan who are separated from their husbands and fathers who are working in the Middle East. The proportion of Indian workers in the Middle East who are living with their families is similarly small and was less than 9 per cent in 1982. Of a total of 800,000 Indian workers in the Middle East, it is estimated that 70,000 of them are living with their families and that these 70,000 have an average of three family members with them in the Middle East. This is in stark contrast to the situation in 1975 when the majority of Indian migrant workers had their families with them. Although no reliable data are available on accompanying family members from East and South-East Asian sending countries, their number is thought to be small.

The Arab countries of the Middle East and North Africa have promoted a new type of international migration, i.e. collective contract migration or project-tied migration. This type of migration is defined by ILO as the movement of foreigners admitted to a migrant-receiving country for a period of time on the basis of a work contract with an enterprise or employer to carry out in that country specific projects that by their nature are limited in time. 16/ Project-tied migration is usually associated with work camps situated away from the population centres. Foreign workers are engaged to put up the buildings and infrastructure. They return home upon completion of their contracts. The use of project-tied Asian labour was initiated by the capital-rich countries in the Middle East in the mid- and late 1970s because it maximized economic efficiency and minimized the social costs of immigration. As a means of keeping down the social costs of migration, most of the receiving countries have introduced restrictions for family migration and make naturalization nearly impossible.

C. South and North America

Although estimates for Latin America date back to 1974, they may safely be assumed to be still valid. The total number of intra-continental migrant workers is estimated to be about 3 million, with about 1.5 million family members (see table 3). The main receiving countries are Argentina, with 1,370,000 migrants, and Venezuela, with 755,000. Brazil, Chile, Colombia and Peru each have migrant populations of over 100,000. The chief emigration countries are Bolivia (with 693,000 workers resident abroad), Paraguay (540,000), Colombia (667,000) and Chile (290,000). Nearly 30 per cent of Paraguay's total population (almost 50 per cent of the active population) reside outside the country; the corresponding figure for Bolivia is around 12 per cent of the total population (40 per cent of the active population). 17/ Most of the movement of workers in the region is illegal migration, much of it occurring in frontier areas that are culturally similar. It is estimated that in recent years illegal movements have increased as a result of widening disparities in economic growth and improvements in transportation and infrastructure.

In the United States of America, it is estimated that there are between 2.5 and 4 million economically active irregular immigrants living in the country, about half coming from Mexico, and 2.5 million legal migrant workers. The other North American receiving country, Canada, admitted 63,000 foreign workers for settlement and 74,375 as non-immigrants in 1980. 17/

D. Africa

South Africa registered a stock of 287,000 black foreign workers in 1980, of whom 220,000 worked in mining and quarrying. During that year, 30,000 white foreigners were also admitted, 43 per cent of whom were economically active. Although substantial numbers of migrant labourers seek seasonal employment in

Table 3. South American region: estimated number of migrant workers in 1974
(Thousands)

Out-migration country	In-migration country										
	Argentina	Bolivia	Brazil	Chile	Colombia	Ecuador	Paraguay	Peru	Uruguay	Venezuela (1961)	Total
Argentina	-	-	-	3	-	-	18	-	25	20	66
Bolivia	500	-	45	70	4	4	-	60	-	10	693
Brazil	70	2	-	-	5	20	30	5	20	20	172
Chile	250	5	-	-	5	-	-	10	-	20	290 a/
Colombia	-	-	-	7	-	50	-	5	-	605	667
Ecuador	-	-	-	8	60	-	-	20	-	20	108
Paraguay	470	-	70	-	-	-	-	-	-	-	540
Peru	-	35	-	40	4	5	-	-	-	20	104
Uruguay	80	-	3	-	-	-	-	-	-	-	83
Venezuela	-	-	-	5	33	-	-	-	-	-	38
Other	-	3	22	2	9	6	2	20	5	40 b/	109
Total	1 370	45	140	135	120	85	50	120	50	755	2 870

Source: International Labour Organisation, "La condition des travailleurs migrants en Amérique du sud", General Conditions of Work Series, No. 31 (Geneva, 1974). The estimates for 1974 have not been changed except for the number of Paraguayans in Argentina, which has dropped by 130,000.

Note: A hyphen indicates that the item is not applicable; no migrants of this nationality have been recorded or estimated, or their magnitude is less than 500.

a/ Excluding about 400,000 economically active border commuters and people of European origin.

b/ Of which 30,000 migrants are from Trinidad and Tobago.

the agricultural sector, relatively little is known about their numbers and origin. Among the sending countries in the region, Lesotho is the most dependent on the export of labour: in 1980, South Africa recruited 151,000 workers from Lesotho. Botswana and Swaziland are relatively small suppliers: in 1979, 19,300 workers were recruited in Botswana by South Africa. 18/

For the past two decades, Malawi and Mozambique have been the major sources of labour for South African mines. However, in 1974, the Government of Malawi dramatically curtailed labour flows to South Africa; after the country had gained independence, the Government of Mozambique took similar steps. These restrictions contributed to the reduction of the total foreign workers in South Africa from 646,504 in 1975 to approximately 302,000 in 1981 (see table 4 below). 19/

Table 4. Employment of foreign Africans by country of origin, 1975-1981

Country	1975	1976	1977	1978	1979	1980	1981
Angola	3 843	805	1 483	341	275	293	69
Botswana	59 835	43 159	43 527	34 665	32 463	29 527	29 169
Lesotho	235 494	160 434	173 882	155 623	152 032	142 329	150 422
Malawi	47 825	12 761	12 413	38 525	35 803	31 824	30 602
Mozambique	250 841	111 257	68 231	49 108	61 550	61 284	59 391
Zimbabwe	13 229	32 716	37 917	27 494	21 547	20 551	16 965
Swaziland	24 703	20 750	18 195	14 054	13 006	12 180	13 418
Zambia	914	766	679	843	809	915	727
Other	9 820	7 162	3 768	6 399	9 224	3 103	995
Total	646 504	389 810	360 095	327 052	326 709	302 006	301 758

Source: Survey of Race Relations (1982), p. 84

A major characteristic of foreign labour in South Africa is the restriction of duration of employment. Generally, the contract period ranges from 6 months to 18 months in the mining industry. Migrant workers from Malawi and Mozambique are usually recruited for 18 months while those from Botswana, Lesotho and Swaziland have contracts for periods ranging from 6 months to 12 months. Recruits from within South Africa usually receive contracts of up to 6 months with possibilities of extension. This category of workers is the only group that has access to mobility from one mine to another. Migrant workers from outside South Africa are restricted to the mines assigned to them in their contracts.

International labour movements in West Africa are subject to less control and are more often spontaneous than movements to South Africa or Europe. The mainstream of migration has been from Burkina Faso, the Gambia, Guinea and Togo to Côte d'Ivoire, Ghana and Senegal. According to ILO estimates, there were about 1.3 million migrant workers in the region in 1980. Côte d'Ivoire is the principal labour-importing country with, according to the 1975 census, 1,425,900 foreign nationals (about 21.3 per cent of the total population). There were an estimated 700,000 migrant workers, who made up about 26 per cent of the total economically active population in the country. In Ghana, there were 562,000 foreign nationals, of whom 55 per cent had come from Togo, 28 per cent from Burkina Faso and 10 per cent from Nigeria. Some 355,000 foreign nationals live in Senegal, according to the most recent estimate of the World Bank. 20/ The largest number of migrants came through the southern borders of the country: about 75,000 from Guinea Bissau and 57,000 from Guinea. Gambia sent about 33,000.

The situation of migrant workers and their families in this region was affected mainly by three developments. First, a substantial reduction in demand for foreign labour in Ghana, as a result of economic difficulties in the early 1970s. The authorities in Ghana had to use the Alien Compliance Order, which required all migrant workers without valid working permits to leave the country, affecting an estimated number of about 300,000 migrants, mainly from Nigeria.

Secondly, a sudden expansion of economic activities in Nigeria during the early 1970s led to a massive employment of foreign labour. Although no exact figures are known, it has been estimated that nearly 2 million migrants were in Nigeria until 1983. Economic difficulties experienced by the country in the early 1980s resulted in administrative measures against migrant labour. Nearly 1.5 million workers, mainly from Ghana, were expelled from the country.

Thirdly, as a result of the steady economic growth of Côte d'Ivoire after 1970, the country attracted a large number of migrants and became the principal labour-importing country in the region.

A special feature of West African migration, which distinguishes it from the southern African pattern, is the duration of stay. In many cases there are no formal agreements between the sending and the receiving countries in the region. Consequently, there is a tendency for a long duration of stay resulting often in permanent residence. Most of the migrants in the subregion are unskilled workers engaged in agriculture and unqualified occupations.

E. Asia

In Oceania in 1980, Australia had 90,000 settler arrivals and New Zealand 42,000. The size of the foreign working populations are not known for that area.

In the Asian region, one of the major labour-importing countries, Singapore, may have more than 175,000 foreign workers, constituting more than 15 per cent of its total labour force. 21/ Approximately 100,000 of these workers come from neighbouring Malaysia and many of the rest are citizens of Indonesia, the Philippines and Thailand. The impact of foreign labour is particularly visible in the case of Singapore's construction workers who are of foreign nationality, mostly Malaysian.

Malaysia is both a major labour exporter and a major labour importer. Only crude estimates are available of the number of migrant workers in Malaysia, but there is no question that the foreign work-force is sizeable. It has been estimated that there are 100,000-300,000 Indonesian migrants in Peninsular Malaysia and another 100,000 in East Malaysia, and 100,000-250,000 Filipinos (including dependants) in Sabah. 22/ A major portion of all these flows consists of illegal or undocumented immigrants, about whom little information is available, and includes both temporary workers who are non-residents and foreign workers who are residents. About 100,000 or more of the foreign workers are classified as non-residents.

F. Conclusion

From this review of the quantitative trends of international labour migration, it can be concluded that the recruitment of foreign workers remains an important factor of the world economy today. The fact that the foreign labour force has not undergone any noticeable reduction during the period of deep recession experienced by market economies in recent years might be seen as evidence that international migration is a long-lasting phenomenon. For many countries it is of vital importance. A number of the labour-importing countries are completely dependent on foreign labour, for example, receiving countries of the Middle East.

In Switzerland, foreigners account for 20 per cent of the active population. In Australia, it is considered that 58 per cent of the country's post-war growth is due to the inflow of foreigners. Among the labour-exporting countries, 25 per cent of the nationals of Botswana and 80 per cent of the nationals of Lesotho are employed abroad. In Bolivia, 13 per cent of the population and 40 per cent of the working population migrated in the mid-1970s; in Paraguay, emigrants account for 28 and 92 per cent of the total and working population, respectively.

The considerable economic significance of international labour migration for the countries concerned has other dimensions. In 1978, the flow of migrant workers' savings to major migrant-sending countries amounted to $US 241,000 million. This provided many developing countries with much-needed hard currency. In Yemen, for example, migrant workers' remittances since the early 1970s have covered the country's growing trade gap and enabled the country to increase its imports correspondingly, which, at the end of the 1970s, amounted to about 600 times the level of exports. On the part of the receiving countries, for example, one in six automobiles made in the Federal Republic of Germany in 1980 can be attributed to the work of migrants from the Mediterranean area.

Although there have been no significant quantitative changes in the international movement of workers since 1975, patterns and conditions of migration have undergone some important modifications. It appears that, in the past 10 years, a new situation has been created in intraregional and interregional movements of workers in the world as a result of the economic crisis that affected all countries, whether industrialized or developing. Among the most significant developments in this field brought about by the economic crisis are: (a) the complete or near stoppage of the traditional movements of workers introduced by major receiving countries; (b) the continuing return of migrant workers to the country of origin; (c) a profound change in the character and scale of labour migration to the high-income oil-exporting countries of the Middle East; (d) an increase in the period of residence of migrants in the host countries; and (e) the overlapping of migratory flows, i.e., certain manpower-exporting countries receive, at the same time, migrant workers from other parts of the world.

In assessing recent trends, the increasing diversity and complexity of international migration for employment is noticeable. Some manifestations of this are:

(a) First, project-tied and similar migration has proved to be a growing form of international migration. Promoted by the Arab countries of the Middle East on an increasing scale, this type of migration seems to be spreading to other regions. Firms from the Republic of Korea negotiated a first contract with the Government of Nigeria. In Asian countries, contractors from the Republic of Korea won more than $1,000 million in new contracts in 1981, compared with less than $300 million in 1980;

(b) Secondly, Western Europe has almost given up the individual contract migration system that was used by migrant-receiving countries over the last two decades. Since the 1973/74 curtailment of the recruitment of workers from abroad, there have been lasting changes in the nature of migration. The closing of frontiers to all new workers has led to a stabilization of the foreign population; the employment of family members living with the immigrant has also contributed to this stabilization. The period of residence of migrants in Western Europe is growing longer. 23/ The number of migrants returning to the country of origin tends to be declining, and there has been an increase in the youngest age groups within the foreign population. The natural surplus of the foreign population is of growing significance;

(c) Thirdly, irregular migration has become a sizeable phenomenon. It is widespread in North and South America and can be found in the Middle East, West Africa, Oceania and Western Europe. With the current global economic difficulties, the interaction between rising pressure to emigrate from poor developing countries and decreasing opportunities for regular migration might well lead to more irregular migration. There are few data on either past or present illegal migration, which makes it impossible to estimate its growth. Nevertheless, there is a broad consensus that there has been a marked increase in undocumented migration. One of the most important effects of illegal migration is the impact on the workers themselves. The unique situation of the unskilled illegal worker may lead to many forms of exploitation, neglect of basic human rights, as well as psychological stress.

II. MAJOR EMERGING PROBLEMS CONCERNING THE WELFARE OF
MIGRANT WORKERS AND THEIR FAMILIES AND MEASURES TO SOLVE THOSE PROBLEMS

A. Legal insecurity

One of the main reasons for the handicaps peculiar to international
migrants is that they are aliens in the country of employment. Migrant workers
are generally rural residents who have been abruptly transplanted to an urban
society. They have to contend not only with ignorance of the new environment,
but also with differences between that environment and the one from which they
have come. In addition, they are subject to certain restrictions. Migrants
can stay only as long as they have the right to work, and they are not free to
look for employment of their choice. The reunion of migrant workers and their
families is still subject to certain direct or indirect administrative
restrictions in most receiving countries, which can delay the admission of the
family for a long period of time or even make it impossible. Above all,
migrants have to face prejudices and discriminatory attitudes on the part of
the population of the receiving country.

In most receiving countries, the status of the foreign worker is
characterized by inequality, which is a cumulation of legal inequality (the
reservation of certain rights for nationals only, such as the right to vote,
the right to work, access to several types of official assistance etc.) and
unequal treatment in practice (when the same rights extend to nationals and
foreign workers but the latter are rarely, if at all, able to fulfil the
conditions). The legal insecurity of migrant workers, resulting from the
temporary character of their residence, combined with the possibility of being
expelled from the host country arbitrarily or unfairly, presents another
source of inequality in practice that adversely affects the social situation
of migrants. The unequal treatment of immigrants is considered to be one of
the major obstacles to their integration in the host country.

On the basis of the analysis made in the present study there is no
evidence to conclude that these basic characteristics of the legal and actual
status of migrant workers and members of their families have been changed in
recent years. As was stated in the reply by the Government of Yugoslavia to
the United Nations questionnaire on the social situation of migrant workers
and their families:

"Concrete examples from life demonstrate that some of the existing
restrictive regulations, as well as failure to comply with the positive
principles established under bilateral and multilateral instruments for
the protection of the status of migrant workers, as well as the
increasingly pronounced xenophobia of late, make the present position of
foreign workers and their families, including Yugoslavs, observed on the
whole, more difficult and uncertain than before."

In its reply, the Government of Yugoslavia gives examples of discriminatory
laws and practices in major receiving countries against migrant workers and
their families. For instance, provisions of the Treaties of Rome concluded
between EEC member States discriminate, both legally and in practice, between
Yugoslav nationals, as well as nationals of other non-member States of the
Community, on the one hand, and the nationals of the country in question and
nationals of other member States of the Community who enjoy equal rights, on
the other hand. The full impact of this discrimination is felt when the right
to work is concerned, because domestic nationals and nationals of EEC member
States are accorded absolute priority over Yugoslav citizens and nationals of
other non-member States of the Community, which means that the latter group of

persons can obtain employment only if there are no domestic applicants or applicants from other EEC member States for a specific vacancy. Yugoslav migrant workers cannot obtain the more attractive and better paid jobs but are often forced to accept hard, underpaid, dirty work involving health hazards and similar disadvantages.

In some receiving countries, the discriminatory attitude towards aliens is based exclusively on domestic regulations. Apart from the numerous requirements that an alien has to comply with in order to obtain certain work or residence permits, especially those ensuring a more favourable status, domestic nationals enjoy priority in employment. Changes of work place or jobs are therefore impossible for a period of many years, which means that foreign workers are precluded from securing better working conditions and pay for themselves over a longer period and thus improving the living conditions of their families.

Actual inequality, which has no basis in either the regulations of the receiving countries or in bilateral and multilateral agreements, but is rather the result of the non-observance, or the inconsistent application, of these agreements and other regulations, is quite widespread, and is manifested in various spheres of the life and work of migrants and their families.

A recently published study on the legal status of immigrant workers in Europe came to such conclusions. 24/ It points out that the way in which lawmakers have traditionally perceived, analysed and determined the status of aliens is compatible neither with the economic realities of the contemporary world nor with the level of economic and social development attained by all Western societies. This state of affairs is ascribed to the fact that the concept of the foreigner underlying all the laws at present in force has remained practically unchanged since the beginning of the century and is based on outdated political and legal principles. The mechanisms controlling migration are too often unsuitable and the status of resident foreigners is marked by too much discrimination.

The following sections of the present study are devoted to an examination of emerging problems, such as the family life of migrants, their adaptation to and integration into the host country, return to and reintegration into the country of origin and the ways in which these problems may be solved, and the adequacy of existing social programmes.

B. The protection of the family

1. Conditions for the reunion of migrant workers and their families

International migration for employment deeply affects the families of migrant workers, which suffer at all stages of migratory life, i.e. emigration from the country of origin, adaptation to and integration into the country of employment and return to and reintegration into the home country. One of the major problems facing migrant workers' families, however, is the difficulty in their reunification.

In a recent United Nations study on regulations for the welfare of migrant workers and their families, the conditions for family reunion have been analysed. 25/ The study concludes that the reunion of migrant workers and their families, although it is not only widely recognized as one of the most important elements contributing to the well-being and integration of migrants into the receiving country, but also provided for by a number of international instruments, is subject to direct or indirect administrative restrictions in most receiving countries that can delay the admission of the migrant worker's family for a long period of time or even make it impossible.

Although the laws and practices of most European receiving countries usually permit spouses and unmarried minor children to accompany or join migrant workers, the reunion of families is still subject to certain conditions that must be met before migrant workers' families are admitted to the country of employment. In some cases, family members are allowed to join migrant workers after a given period of time, usually one year. Some countries of employment require family members to be in good health. In most countries, migrant workers are required to show that they have sufficient resources to maintain a family or that adequate housing is available for them. Recently, further restrictions have been imposed by some countries; for example, a limitation on the age of the children whom foreign workers may bring into the receiving countries has been introduced in some countries.

In most of Africa, both sending and receiving countries permit migrant workers to be accompanied by their families. The only exception is South Africa, where women and children from Lesotho, Malawi, Swaziland, Zimbabwe and other labour-supplying States are prohibited from living with migrant workers, except in very rare situations. 26/ For example, it is reported that in Lesotho alone, according to the 1976 census, 40 to 60 per cent of the married women are wives of absentee migrants. 27/ In some of the labour agreements between African countries, only workers are entitled to transportation to the place of work; workers have the right to live with their families in the receiving countries, but they must bear the expense themselves. Owing to the fact that contracts are generally for six months to two years, most workers do not take their families with them unless they decide to settle in the receiving country for a period of time after the expiration of the contract. The migrant workers themselves are responsible for taking the proper legal steps should they decide to remain in the host country after the end of the contract (Cameroon, Côte d'Ivoire, Gabon).

Legislation relating to migrant workers in the major receiving countries of Latin America sets no limitations to the entry and stay of the families of immigrants who are authorized to work and reside in the country of employment. Migrant workers and members of their families enjoy full equality of treatment with the national population regarding access to social services according to national legislation. The minor children of the migrant workers have the right to work when they reach the working age prescribed by the legislation of the country of immigration. Family reunification is facilitated by the similarity of climates, languages and customs and the presence of many compatriots.

Most receiving countries of the Middle East have adopted a policy of restricting family immigration and employing migrant workers on fixed-term contracts, with repatriation upon expiration of those contracts. In Saudi Arabia, for example, with the exception of nationals of Democratic Yemen and Yemen, who are given four-year residence permits upon arrival, all foreign workers must have a Saudi sponsor. Workers may not change employers without obtaining a release from their previous employer, and then they must leave the country and re-apply for a visa. In 1980, the Government took further steps to reinforce control over foreigners. Apart from certain categories of professional workers, all foreigners were prohibited from bringing their wives and children and many families already in the country were required to leave.

Having temporary residence, migrants cannot personally obtain visas for relatives or friends to visit them. This applies even to immediate family

members. Any permits for the visits of friends or relatives have to be
applied for by migrants' guarantors, whereby the guarantors will be officially
guaranteeing the visitors of their employees. Since 1980, visiting permits
have become harder to obtain even for applications presented by guarantors be
they citizens or corporations.

More serious are the rules on the admission of immediate family members
to join migrant workers. In order to obtain residence permits for their
families, migrant workers have to present a house lease or contract and
evidence that their monthly income is above a certain level. This rule
virtually deprives at least 80 per cent of the migrant workers of the
possibility of having their families even join them and applies even to a
single worker who marries while working in the Middle East. 28/

Another major problem faced by earlier migrants who were able to obtain
residence for their families before the mid-seventies, or those who formed
families within the host country, is that of family residence. According to
the receiving countries' legal definition, "family residence" is granted only
to parents, wife and children under 21 years of age. Upon reaching the age of
21, the children of a migrant are considered as adults, lose their family
residence and must obtain a residence permit on their own or leave the country.

Governments of receiving countries in Western Asia have shown little
interest in the past 30 years in naturalizing migrant workers, even those who
are nationals of a country in the region or who are in technical and professional
occupations. For instance, Kuwait naturalized only 60,000 migrants during the
period 1971-1980, most of whom were Bedouins who had been residing in Kuwait for
more than 50 years rather than classical "migrant labour", of whom less than
5,000 were naturalized. Out of the 350,000 Palestinians residing in Kuwait, less
than 400 were naturalized. 29/ Moreover, in April 1984, the Kuwaiti parliament
passed a resolution allowing the Government to naturalize no more than 500 migrant
workers annually, provided they had rendered great services to Kuwait. 30/

The Migrant Workers Recommendation, 1975, of ILO (No. 151, paragraph 13)
provides that:

"All possible measures should be taken both by countries of employment
and by countries of origin to facilitate the reunification of families of
migrant workers as rapidly as possible. These measures should include,
as necessary, national laws or regulations and bilateral and multilateral
arrangements."

However, according to a 1980 ILO report, 31/ only a limited number of measures
designed to facilitate family reunification were mentioned in the replies by
Governments to the above-mentioned questionnaire. Some countries stated in
general terms that the immigration authorities were responsible for facilita-
ting the entry of migrant workers' families; others referred to financial
assistance for the transport costs of the family members.

In most receiving countries, regulations and practices concerning family
reunion are still governed mainly by considerations of a political and
economic nature, such as reluctance to increase the foreign segment of the
population or to burden the national social security system, and the need of
industry for mobile and cheap labour. Regrettably, the humanitarian factor,
namely, the protection of the migrant worker's right to a normal family life
is still not a decisive one in all policies involving family reunion.

As was suggested in a recent United Nations report to the Commission for Social Development,

"In order to encourage the reunion of families of migrant workers, specific measures should be envisaged, through bilateral, multilateral agreements and national legislative documents, based on the recognition that, once a worker has been admitted to the country and granted residence, efforts should be made to eliminate any obstacles to family reunion. Such measures should include: (a) recognition by national legislation in the receiving country of the right of the migrant worker to be reunited with his family; (b) the setting of a maximum waiting period; and (c) prompt examination of applications for admission of the family, so that the foreign worker is not left too long in ignorance of the outcome of his application." 32/

2. Families left behind in the country of origin

In most cases, the international migration of workers is associated with the separation of families, the spouse and children or only the children being left behind in the country of origin. Family members remaining in countries of origin are confronted with a number of problems. Children are often left with members of their families who, in many cases, are not in a position to give them the kind of help they would have received from their fathers and mothers. When one parent emigrates, the other parent has to take on additional responsibilities for the family, and as a result the education of the children might be sacrificed to other preoccupations.

According to some estimates, in European sending countries alone nearly 2 million children have remained behind when the father or both parents work abroad. 33/ Although in recent years the process of migrant family reunion has been much stronger than before, the majority of the members of the families of migrant workers stay in the country of origin. For example, in Yugoslavia, over two thirds of the members of families of workers temporarily employed abroad, covered by the population census in 1981, were resident in the home country.

(a) Abuses in recruitment

It is important to note that in many sending countries, potential migrants and members of their families face problems at the stage of recruitment. A common shortfall is the lack of reliable and comprehensive information about working and living conditions in the receiving countries. Another problem is that of recruitment abuses, which have been rather routine throughout Asia because of the lack of strong government controls and the intense interest of workers in obtaining foreign employment. The proliferation of private recruiting agents has made government oversight a more difficult task. In the Philippines, about 450 recruiters, 200 contractors, and 200 manning agents are involved in overseas employment. In Thailand, recruitment involves 600 or more firms, most of which are not registered with the Labour Department.

Abuses have been particularly flagrant in the imposition of recruitment fees that are charged to the workers. Although most countries limit the amount of the fees that can be assessed, overcharges are common. Illegal fees are most likely to be charged to workers holding individual visas.

Abuses are also rife in the area of trade testing. For a price, workers who do not have appropriate skills may be certified as qualified. Bribes may also be exacted from workers by government officials who issue emigration documents and other official papers.

In most countries, legislation already exists to control these abuses, but its enforcement is often lax. Workers who do obtain legitimate jobs abroad are unlikely to complain about illegal fees for fear of losing their jobs. Others who are cheated by recruiters may be reluctant to file official complaints out of fear of reprisals, or because they are not convinced that the Government will take any action. Illegal recruiters or those who charge excessive fees are often protected by corrupt government officials.

Prospective migrant workers face a lengthy process of approvals that involves an unusual amount of red tape. The application process is particularly burdensome for workers from outlying areas who often spend several months processing papers in a large city and therefore cannot easily hold a permanent job during that time. In the Philippines, for example, the waiting time between application for the first job overseas and actual departure is 3 months or less for most workers, but 27 per cent of the applicants have to wait for 4-6 months, 13 per cent for 7-12 months and 3 per cent for more than 12 months. 34/ Applicants who have to borrow money at high interest rates to finance the cost of applying for foreign employment are particularly disadvantaged. In the Philippines, one study reported that 24 per cent of Middle East workers needed to borrow money and in Thailand almost 50 per cent of the costs of obtaining a foreign job were financed either by borrowing or by selling property. Since the monthly interest on such borrowed money is high, the failure to obtain foreign employment can sometimes lead to bankruptcy and loss of property. 35/

Despite the difficulty of stemming illegal recruitment, some progress is being made. In the Philippines, the National Council on Illegal Recruitment has spearheaded a campaign to curtail illegal activities. In 1983, the Ministry of Labour and Employment resolved 804 cases of illegal recruitment in the Philippines and suspended or cancelled the licences of 44 recruiting agencies. 36/ The Philippine Overseas Employment Administration has also held anti-illegal recruitment seminars in several locations throughout the country. Indian workers with complaints can go to the Protector General of Emigration in the Ministry of Labour and Rehabilitation. At New Delhi, there is a "May I help you" counter that provides information to overseas workers and receives complaints about recruiting agents. Bangladesh has a provision that special courts to deal with infractions of the 1983 Emigration Ordinance should be set up. All of these efforts, however, have not been able to eliminate continuing problems in the recruitment process.

(b) Women and children left behind in the country of origin

Reasons for remaining in the country of origin are complicated and differ according to the country and family. The choice to remain can be seen from two perspectives: first, it can have a negative origin in the sense that the family is not allowed to join the man in the receiving country or that the woman will not be allowed to work there, or that the legal or economic position of the man is so uncertain as to prevent his family from joining him. Secondly, the receiving country make such requirements of migrants who want to bring their families as to make family reunification virtually impossible.

As a recent report of the Council of Europe indicates, 37/ the lives of women who remain in the country of origin while their husbands, fathers or sons migrate are certainly changed by the separation. The departure of male members of a family and of a community will in several ways upset and change the social organization. Long separation will affect the traditional division of labour, as well as parental roles, and also the economic situation of the women left behind. The duration of separation, as well as the prospects for family reunification in the receiving country or in the country of origin, influence the possibilities for women to cope with family separation. Women will also be affected differently according to their socio-economic environment.

However, the absence of men tends to make women more dependent on the financial contributions because of the disruption of the local economy caused by male out-migration. Disruption also occurs on a cultural and ideological level, as the culture and prevailing values in the receiving country are inserted between the members of the family and the local community.

Women who remain in communities that have been drained of most of the male population of working age find themselves in deteriorating economic circumstances, and become increasingly dependent on the income that is being transmitted from workers in other countries. When this transfer of income is stopped, women find themselves in a more dependent position than before. The question of the development of local economies, which are affected by migration, is of concern also to the remaining women who need an economic base for the maintenance and upbringing of their children.

Although the situation of children left behind in the country of origin has not been studied sufficiently, case studies undertaken in sending countries give an idea of the nature of the problems faced by these children. A study covering 100 Tunisian families left at home reveals that some children suffer from such disorders as poor school performance, backwardness, unruliness, absenteeism, lack of attention and difficult relationships with teachers and pupils. 38/ There is evidence that separation hampers the development of children and handicaps them in their school work. The absence of the parents leaves a gap that cannot be completely filled by others, which may have undesirable consequences: poor social adjustment, weakness of character and a feeling of isolation and emotional solitude.

However, the divorce of the parents owing to the emigration of one spouse may have even more serious effects on the children. According to a United Nations report on the welfare of migrant workers and their families, migration led to a divorce between the parents in 10 per cent of the families studied in Serbia (the average divorce rate in Serbia was 1.5 per cent). 39/ In some large villages in Serbia, the divorce rate among migrants even amounted to 28 per cent. In Croatia alone over a two-year period, 1,298 divorces were registered each divorce involving minor children and at least one spouse who had been or was working abroad.

In Asian sending countries, where few migrant workers bring their families with them during their overseas assignments, there has been a growing interest in studying the effect of the absence of migrant workers on the members of their families left behind. The effect is considered to be wide ranging, covering such areas as family cohesion, marital stability, the status of women, education, disciplinary and emotional problems.

In terms of family cohesion, for example, some studies conclude that despite the adverse impact of the husband's absence, the families of Asian migrant workers generally cope rather well with their new situation. The supportive role of the extended family is crucial to the adjustment process. The families that are left behind place great reliance on the kinship group for help and advice. All the evidence indicates that there is increased interdependence among family members while the worker is away. Several studies have concluded that labour migration has had the effect of reinforcing kin networks and strengthening the extended family system. 40/ In India and Pakistan, labour migration has also resulted in an increase in joint family living arrangements; in Pakistan, 96 per cent of the families with foreign labour migrants reportedly live in extended families, compared with 55 per cent of all Pakistani families. 41/

The absence of the husband can put strains on a marriage, but reports of marital dissolution and infidelity owing to labour migration appear to be overrated. There is little reliable evidence that the institution of marriage has been adversely affected by foreign labour migration. In the State of Kerala, India, it was found that there was an unprecedentedly high rate of divorce and petitions for legal separation, but it is difficult to attribute this solely to labour migration. In Bangladesh, a few cases of young married migrants divorcing their wives to marry into families with a higher status were reported. Data from four companies in the Republic of Korea indicate that 8.6 per cent of the grievances filed with the company counselling centres concerned unfaithful wives, 42/ but these complaints involved only a small number of workers. In general, the incidence of family problems is quite low. One of the most careful studies of this issue, based on both community informants and a sample survey of the wives of migrant workers, was conducted in the Philippines. 43/ This study found little support for the claim that foreign employment has resulted in the break-up of marriages and also found that instances of infidelity were rare and that, in any case, infidelity could not be definitely attributed to overseas employment.

It might be assumed that in the husband's absence the wife would take on new responsibilities and be able to take advantage of new opportunities that could increase her status in the family and the community. However, the evidence on whether or not labour migration is an "emancipating" experience for wives who are left behind is mixed. In Pakistan, the wives of foreign contract workers become more independent and mature after their husbands leave, but they rely on their parents-in-law and brothers-in-law for making important decisions, such as the purchase of property, the children's education, household purchases and financial investments. There is only a small gain in the wives' decision-making power since women rarely have direct control over remittances: only 17 per cent of the bank drafts for foreign remittances are made out in the wife's name. 44/ Changes in women's responsibilities are more evident in India: wives of overseas Indian workers often manage the day-to-day household budget while their husbands are abroad, but tend to seek advice from relatives on the repayment of debts or the management of savings. The wives have started to manage their own bank accounts and banks are beginning to cater to their needs. In villages with large numbers of Muslims working overseas, some banks have opened special counters where Muslim women can be served without being seen by male customers. In the Philippines, where women have a relatively high status, it was found that the husband's absence often helps to foster the personal development of the women who are left behind. 43/ Women take on new responsibilities and they are perceived to handle these responsibilities quite well.

Families that receive remittances from migrant workers are able to spend more on their children's education, but there is conflicting evidence about the effects of overseas migration on schooling. Among Filipinos working in the Middle East, 21.6 per cent said that the education of their children was the primary object they wanted to achieve before returning home. The monthly household expenditure for education rose from an average of 184 Philippine pesos before the migrant worker left for the Middle East to 499 pesos afterwards. School enrolment also appears to have increased for the children of migrant workers in India and Pakistan.

The effect of labour migration on education is not entirely positive, however. In many cases, education (particularly academic training) is seen as being superfluous since young persons think they can obtain jobs abroad without a substantial amount of formal education. The Philippines has experienced problems with young school drop-outs who want to work in the Middle East. Several studies in Pakistan have found a lack of interest in education because of work opportunities in the Middle East, and in Bangladesh, the education of children has suffered in migrant households because of a lack of paternal supervision.

Concern about disciplinary problems and the difficulty of raising children in the absence of the father have been pointed out in research in Pakistan, the Philippines and the Republic of Korea. About 70 per cent of Philippine wives reported that they found the care and discipline of their children burdensome in the absence of their husbands. In Bangladesh and Pakistan, the migrants themselves had mixed views about problems of discipline among their children, but they were concerned that their children seemed to have become more self-indulgent, spendthrift, and careless about their education.

The incidence of serious problems, such as juvenile delinquency and drug addiction, differs; in the State of Kerala, substantial juvenile delinquency was found among children of migrant families.

Among the most negative consequences of the separation of families are the emotional and psychological problems that wives of migrants endure. Mental illness has been found to be particularly acute in the so-called "Gulf pockets" of the State of Kerala, and women aged from 15 to 25 years seem to be the major victims. A main reason for psychiatric disorders is the incompatibility of these young women with their husbands' parents, which is made worse by the absence of their husbands. Similarly, it was reported in Pakistan that the head of the psychology department in a hospital near Islamabad dealt every day with 10 to 15 patients afflicted with what has been termed as the "Dubai syndrome". Over a six-month period, about 1,450 such patients were treated in one hospital alone. The patients suffered from a variety of psychosomatic illness, and the younger patients experienced a high degree of sexual frustration. 45/

Many studies undertaken on the situation of separated families in Burkina Faso, Lesotho, Swaziland and the United Republic of Tanzania have shown that migration from poorer households has left families vulnerable to crisis and tends to restrict their production capabilities. It also leads to situations where women, children and old people are obliged to take over work that is usually done by young and adult males, such as agricultural tasks.

(c) Remittances

Measures taken by the countries concerned on behalf of families and children left behind in the country of origin have been designed to ensure that they are taken care of materially. Practically all bilateral agreements between labour-exporting and importing countries include provisions on the transfer of the remittances to migrant workers' families. In some countries, the remittance of a fixed percentage of the salary of migrant workers to their families is mandatory. For example, average Asian workers in the Middle East remit more than 50 per cent (and often as much as 70-90 per cent) of their total earnings to their families.

Remittances from migrant workers have undeniably raised the standard of living of the households of foreign workers. In Pakistan, for example,

nutritional levels improved markedly in households with emigrants. In the
Philippines, 64 per cent of migrant workers acquired luxuries, such as
television sets, video cassette recorders and stereo equipment after their
overseas employment, and 60 per cent acquired appliances, such as refrigerators
and stoves. In Thailand, 41 per cent of a sample of foreign workers had
purchased stereo equipment, 37 per cent an electric fan, 29 per cent a
television set, 24 per cent a refrigerator and 18 per cent a sewing machine.
While some of these goods would have been purchased even if the worker had not
accepted an overseas assignment, most of the luxuries would not have been
affordable without a source of foreign income.

In Asia, as in other parts of the world, the largest part of the
remittance (50-70 per cent) is spent on current consumption, particularly on
food, clothing and household goods. Apart from consumption, the major
expenditure is the purchase of land and the construction or improvement of
housing. Housing investments not only improve the physical comfort of the
family, but also increase the family's status with relatives and in the
community as a whole. Remittances are also spent on the education of household
members and the payment of debt. Among a small sample of Bangladeshis working
in Saudi Arabia, 17 per cent of non-consumption remittances was spent on the
repayment of debt. A substantial proportion of remittances also goes towards
retirement and the payment of debt in the Philippines. Before going abroad,
26 per cent of all Filipinos working overseas were in debt, but after their
return only 15 per cent were in debt. Only about 10 per cent of remittances
are normally spent on productive investment in physical assets.

One reason for the lack of investment out of remittances is the dearth of
viable investment opportunities, particularly in rural areas. To counteract
this problem, a few Asian Governments have established programmes to divert
remittances to productive uses. Pakistan has an investment programme to try
to induce overseas workers to invest in industrial projects, particularly in
the Karachi Export Processing Zone. Bangladesh, Pakistan, and the Republic of
Korea all have attractive housing schemes for overseas workers. Bangladesh,
India, Pakistan and Sri Lanka all allow migrant workers to maintain foreign
currency bank accounts. Finally, Bangladesh has developed special incentive
schemes for overseas workers, such as the Wage Earners' Development Bonds. 46/

In Africa, dependence on and regularity of remittances vary from one
country to another. The level of dependence is much higher in countries where
population density and lack of land are high. In Lesotho, for example, as
many as 90 per cent of all emigrant households are completely dependent on
remittances. About two thirds of them reported that they were not even
receiving enough money to live on, because of the irregularities in remittances.
It is obvious that the welfare of the migrants' families who are left behind
suffers as a result.

(d) Child allowances

Another part of the income of families remaining in the country of origin
is child allowances, which are transferred in accordance with bilateral and
multilateral agreements. In accordance with the Nordic Council's first
convention on social security, Denmark, Finland, Iceland, Norway and Sweden
pay family allowances at the same rate, whether or not the children reside in
the Nordic Council country in which the migrant works. The same principle
applies in regulations concerning foreign workers belonging to States members
of the EEC, with some exceptions. France, for example, pays family allowances
at the rate prevailing in the country of origin. The difference is made up by
a Social Action Fund, which was set up in 1958 to promote housing and

educational and vocational training activities for migrants in the host
country. France also has bilateral agreements with Greece, Morocco, Portugal,
Spain, Yugoslavia and a number of African countries. Under the agreements,
family allowances are paid at the rate prevalent in those countries. For
certain countries, the payment of French allowances is limited to four
children. In other countries (Portugal, Spain, Yugoslavia), payment is made
from the second child onwards, corresponding to the conditions for the family
allowances entitlement in France. In the Federal Republic of Germany, family
allowances for children left behind have been considerably reduced since 1975.
Since 1980, allowances are no longer paid for children remaining in Turkey. In
the United Kingdom of Great Britain and Northern Ireland, family allowances are
not transferrable to children left behind. In the Netherlands, all migrants
have the right to transfer family allowances to their children living outside
the Netherlands. Under bilateral agreements concluded between Switzerland and
Greece, Italy, Spain and Turkey and allowances can be transferred to children
in the countries of origin if the father is an agricultural worker or a small
farmer. Yugoslav workers can transfer allowances, which are the same amount
as Swiss nationals receive, to all their children.

In Africa, family benefits are generally granted only for children
residing in the country where the worker is employed. In some cases,
surviving dependants may even lose all entitlement to pensions for employment
injuries if they were living outside the receiving country at the time of
injury. As regards disability, old age and general survivor's pensions, the
laws in many countries prescribe the suspension of benefits if the recipient
ceases to reside in that country. The difficulties encountered by the
migrants and their families when benefits are suspended can be easily seen.

In Latin America, in accordance with the agreements concluded by
Argentina with Chile (1971) and Uruguay (1974) on social security, family
allowances are paid to migrant workers only if their families live with them
in the country of employment. The same principle is applied in bilateral
agreements concluded between Chile and Paraguay.

Discrepancies can be seen in the treatment of children of migrant
workers, in which those left in the home country are often not entitled to
receive the same benefits as those who live with their parents abroad. The
apparent inequality of treatment seems particularly unfair in view of the
completely equal treatment of migrant workers with regard to taxes and social
security contributions, which are ultimately aimed at meeting the needs of all
their children.

(e) Social protection

In most countries of origin, the families of migrant workers can benefit
from the services that are available to the population as a whole. Little has
been done, however, for the social protection of migrants. Yugoslavia seems
to be the only country that has taken specific measures in this direction.
According to the law on the basic conditions of temporary employment and
protection of Yugoslav citizens working abroad and other legal and administrative regulations adopted on the basis of that law, workers seeking employment
abroad must first obtain from the Yugoslav Employment Office a guarantee that
the members of their families left behind will be looked after materially and
that their children will be brought up normally. In addition, efforts have
been made to improve bilateral and multilateral instruments with a view to
simplifying procedures for migrants to meet their material obligations towards
their families left in the country of origin (payment of living allowances to
mothers and children, sickness insurance etc.).

In most Asian and Latin American sending countries, national legislation and regulations and bilateral agreements say nothing about the rights that should be enjoyed by the members of separated families. There is no assistance that mothers and children can rely on to ensure that migrant workers will continue to discharge their material obligations from the host country; the remittance of money remains a matter of the goodwill and sense of responsiblity of the worker.

The lack of funds and the need to meet the more pressing needs of the population at large often prevent countries of origin from taking specific measures to deal with the social problems of the families of migrant workers left behind. With regard to the welfare of families left behind, a number of problems deserve consideration: (a) the hardship involved for families when remittances are irregular or fail altogether; (b) the judicious use of the income derived from work abroad to meet immediate and long-term needs of the migrant workers' family; (c) information regarding social security and other rights, and assistance in claiming benefits; (d) communication with the authorities and the migrant worker abroad; and (e) the rearing of children, family counselling etc. More organized efforts will be needed on the part of sending countries to deal with these problems.

3. Migrant families in the country of residence

Despite difficulties, a large proportion of migrant workers do reunite with their families in the country of employment. It was estimated in 1973 that at least half of the married migrants in European receiving countries lived with their families. It is reasonable to believe that this proportion could be larger at present because, since the 1973 freeze on the recruitment of people who are not nationals of EEC countries, authorities in major European countries of employment have permitted family reunion, although with certain limitations.

After a period of separation, families of migrant workers often have to adjust to a new, strange and sometimes hostile environment. The migrant family is affected by isolation and loneliness, and language problems restrict opportunities of becoming acquainted with the culture and customs of the host country. Because the main concerns of migrants are employment and earnings, educational opportunities take secondary place.

One of the problems stressed by some researchers is the different rates at which family members adapt themselves to a new society. It has been noted that children adapt more easily than their parents to a new culture. As a consequence of this and other factors of migrant life, migrant parents have less control over their children than their local neighbours, and much less than they would have had in the country of origin. 47/ As a result, the bonds between parents and children are weakened. The children often have no interest in, or sometimes openly reject, the "inferior" culture of the parents, which can lead to a lack of communication or even conflict between generations. Problems of communication in families are considered to be very serious. If both parents are working, they have too little time to deal with their adolescent children's problems. Special difficulties may arise because young people cannot find work or have no vocational training; as a result, many young people leave the family circle.

The relationship between husbands and wives also changes as a result of the new situation in the country of employment. The data on difficulties with reunification indicate that after a long separation, the husband, who has gained independence, may find it difficult to readjust to family life. The wife sometimes is confronted with ambiguous expectations from her husband, who would like to see her both maintain the submissive position that she occupies in the patriarchal family and, at the same time, behave in a more liberated way, as many women in the host country do. These feelings may result in further estrangement of the marital partners and end in dissolution of the relationship. As a consequence, family separation, as well as family reunion, provokes family crises, which some families manage to overcome, but others do not. 47/

Migrants' wives have special problems. Wives have to adapt to cultural patterns in the broad sense, such as the life-style, family planning practices etc., as well as language of the country of employment. In household tasks, wives have to cope with different foods and different patterns of consumption. However, the most pronounced problem confronting wives is social isolation in the host country. The social isolation of migrant wives is considered to be much larger than that of husbands or children, who are integrated through their work or schools. Wives from some Moslem countries find themselves in an especially difficult situation: in the home country they were integrated into an extended family and in Europe they live in a nuclear family. As a result, in addition to some hardships common to all migrants, these wives have the sole responsibility for the household and the care of the children, while in their home countries they were accustomed to sharing such responsibilities with other women.

In addition to the internal problems of the migrant family in the country of employment noted above, the family as a group has to cope with external factors, i.e., its integration into society in terms of housing, culture, social welfare services, schooling for the children etc. Some of these factors, such as housing and social welfare services, have been given much attention in international studies. 48/ Other factors will be described in the next chapter. It should be stressed that many migrant families can be categorized as deprived families; many of their problems are inherent in this social group and, in addition, aggravated by cultural differences and discrimination.

Some researchers who have analysed programmes for migrant workers in receiving countries point out that the specific problems of the migrant family as a unit have not been given proper attention in these programmes, which are designed to integrate migrants as individuals and not as family units. In recent years, a number of measures have been taken for the integration of migrant workers' children, but there are no comprehensive policies and programmes designed to facilitate the integration of migrant families.

There is an apparent lack of systematic studies and research on migrant families. As a result, the migrant family to some extent remains an unknown quantity for policy makers. A number of scientific studies of migrant workers and their children are available, and an increasing number are devoted to women migrants, but there is little mention of the migrant family in all this literature. The fact that researchers are not interested in the migrant family indicates that neither the public nor officials have become properly aware of the family as a specific phenomenon associated with migration for purposes of work.

Some reasons for the lack of interest might be:

(a) That from the point of view of the labour market, the industrialized countries are interested in workers, not in families. Families and family reunion could run counter to the policy of rotating workers in different locations;

(b) That from a sociological point of view, the family is not directly involved in such important areas of social conflict as employment and schooling;

(c) That an evaluation of the migrant family is affected by the general socio-political situation in the receiving country, where often the family no longer has a proper place in society.

Churches and some non-governmental organizations have been active in recent years in attracting the attention of the Governments of receiving countries to the specific problems of migrant families. They maintain that the individualistic approach to the integration of migrants pursued by some receiving countries is inconsistent with a realistic integration policy. The family is not a group of individuals, but an ethnic group and, as such, should be included in the integration process. Unless the migrants' family are taken into account, there can be no effective integration policy. 49/

In this sense, international organizations dealing with the welfare of migrant workers and their families, whether governmental or non-governmental, have an important role to play in drawing the attention of researchers and social planners in sending and receiving countries to the problems confronting the migrant family at all stages of the so-called "migratory-chain", in order to provide Governments with policy options designed to protect families as a fundamental unit of society.

Responsible government authorities should pay more attention to the elimination of obstacles that may impede reunification of migrant workers' families and their integration into the host society. Possible actions in this respect might be:

(a) Initiating measures of a legal nature (mentioned above), recognizing the right of migrant workers to be reunited with their families;

(b) Developing major constructive programmes in accordance with the country's needs, and taking into consideration the specific needs of migrant workers and their families; guaranteeing migrant workers equality of treatment with national workers with regard to access to state-subsidized housing; and providing financial facilities wherever possible for low-cost housing for migrant workers and their families;

(c) Improving infrastructural services, such as education facilities for children of migrant workers, taking into account their specific needs; proper information and reception structures for families, including facilities for leisure-time activities for family members; social security provisions, such as family allowances; and maternity grants or health insurance for family members;

(d) Providing financial assistance in the form of either the partial payment of the family travel costs or an allowance to offset the additional expenses incurred by the family's arrival.

C. Adaptation to and integration into the country of employment

1. Social and occupational integration of young migrants

In Europe, in spite of the fact that there has been slow but steady progress in recent years towards improving the economic and social position of migrant workers and their families, there are still many problems to be

solved. One of the most serious problems is the social integration of the
estimated 7 million children of migrant workers presently living in Western
Europe. These young people, who account for an increasing share of school-
children in the major European countries of employment, have found themselves
in increasingly difficult situations. As a recent OECD study notes, the home
and social environment and de facto status of many young people do not
encourage them to profit fully from the education and training they might
receive. Thus, young workers of foreign origin are currently the most
vulnerable of all demographic groups to unemployment. 50/ In addition, in
recent studies, they have been described as rootless because they feel foreign
both in their country of residence and in the country of origin.

Shortcomings in the education of foreign children have been studied by
various research institutes in major receiving countries in Europe, as well as
by international organizations, and have been described in many reports. In
general, these shortcomings include the following:

(a) First, there is a lack of education at the pre-school level. All of
the data available in major European receiving countries reveal that the
majority of migrant children do not receive any pre-school education. For
example, according to a report prepared by Turkey for the Tripartite Technical
Seminar on Second Generation Migrants, held at Lisbon in 1981, in the context
of a United Nations Development Programme/ILO European regional project, only
28 per cent of the children of Turkish migrants in the Federal Republic of
Germany go to kindergarten, compared with 70 per cent of the children of
nationals of the Federal Republic of Germany. Moreover, the effectiveness of
pre-school education is to a great extent diminished by the fact that special
language training programmes for migrant children in kindergarten are poorly
developed, particularly with respect to the mother tongue of the child. This
negatively affects the child's ability to learn the language of the receiving
country, as well as the child's pride and self-esteem;

(b) Secondly, although as a rule national legislation on compulsory
schooling in the receiving country applies to children of migrant workers, a
large number of migrant children of compulsory school age do not continue
their education at all, for various reasons. Their number was estimated to be
300,000 in 1975. 51/ Although the situation with respect to compulsory
education of immigrant children has improved in recent years, it is far from
satisfactory. In the Federal Republic of Germany, 20 per cent of migrant
children do not comply with compulsory schooling regulations; 52/

(c) Thirdly, migrant children who receive compulsory education usually
perform poorly. In the Federal Republic of Germany, according to official
data, more than half of all foreign children fail to earn a post-primary
education certificate. 53/ The percentages vary according to the child's
nationality, as well as to the regions of the country. Research on Greek
immigrants conducted recently in the Federal Republic of Germany revealed that
only 36 per cent of their children succeeded in gaining a leaving certificate
of primary education (Hauptschule), compared with 80 per cent of the children
from the Federal Republic of Germany. In Berlin (West) some 90 per cent of
the children of migrant workers do not finish their post-primary education. 54/
Migrant children are over-represented in those types of education that are
usually offered to the educationally disadvantaged. For example, in Yugoslavia,
children in special teaching establishments or in the special classes at normal
schools account for 3 per cent of the total number of pupils, while 14.5 per cent
of Yugoslav children living abroad are in special classes or establishments. 55/
In Sweden, foreign children from Mediterranean countries who continued their
education in the seventh grade represented 12.6 per cent of all pupils in the

school year 1978/79, but accounted for about 20 per cent of all pupils in special education. 56/ In addition, earlier research has shown that a large proportion of foreign children were placed in classes with younger children, which slows the development and limits the educational achievements of the foreign children.

Owing to the high scholastic failure rate in compulsory school, the percentage of immigrant children enrolled in secondary education is much lower than that of native children. In France, 80 per cent of foreign children have to repeat a year in schools where they are oriented towards continuation on to secondary schooling, while the corresponding figure for French children is 48 per cent. 57/ In Belgium, according to a recent study, only 30 per cent of the foreign children who complete their studies in the compulsory schools continue their education in the upper-secondary schools. In the Federal Republic of Germany, only 6 per cent of foreign children follow secondary education (the Realschule or Gymnasium). In Sweden, approximately 80 per cent of all pupils continue their education in secondary school, after nine years of comprehensive school, compared with 69 per cent of immigrant children. 58/ A high rate of scholastic failure has been revealed in France, where 20 out of 100 foreign children leave school at the age of 16, unable to read or write French; 60 per cent have great difficulties in school or irremediable learning problems; and only 20 per cent may be regarded as having had a normal schooling. 59/

In recent years, evident progress has been made in the education of children of migrant workers in most European receiving countries. For example, Member States have taken action to promote the language and culture of the country of origin. In Norway, State funds have been made available since 1982 to co-finance the recruitment of mother-tongue teachers for kindergartens where at least four foreign children speak the same language. In Switzerland, experiments are being made with "mixed kindergartens" in which language teaching is often a feature, designed to achieve the integration of pupils and to safeguard their cultural identity. In Luxembourg, classes in the mother tongue of pupils were introduced into the curriculum in the autumn of 1983. In the Netherlands, parliament is considering an amendment to the Primary Education Act; following its finalization and adoption, tuition in the mother tongue, as requested by foreign parents for their children, and as provided in practice, will be placed on an official footing.

In Sweden, the schemes introduced before 1980 are developing remarkably: in 600 classes, tuition is entirely in the mother tongue, and the new compulsory schooling curriculum that recently came into force includes among possible subjects further cultural studies. In addition, a general report entitled "Reform of the upper secondary school" was presented in October 1981, which included several proposals to facilitate the study by pupils of foreign origin of their mother tongue. However, measures taken so far have been insufficient compared with the educational needs of immigrant children. Foreign children are not able to enjoy equality of opportunity in education for the following reasons: (a) the low socio-economic origin of immigrant children, whose parents are mainly unskilled workers; (b) the cultural conflicts that the migrants' children experience in the society of the receiving country; and (c) the constant insecurity felt by immigrant families in the receiving countries in terms of employment and residence.

In addition, migrant children are at a disadvantage because the educational system is not fully adapted to their educational needs. The educational system is influenced by the uncertainty about the ultimate goal of the education of children of migrants, i.e. is the system aimed at integrating foreign children into the receiving country, preparing them for eventual return to the country of origin, or at giving them a kind of "life insurance" by preparing them for life in both countries?

The goal is generally viewed as providing migrant children with a genuine opportunity for integration into the host country while preserving close ties with the country of origin in order to make reintegration easier should they return to the country of origin. Moreover, research findings enable policy makers to understand fully the rationale of teaching in the mother tongue of the child, which is now considered not only as a vitally important element of education in case of eventual return to the country of origin, but also as a tool for counteracting poor educational performance. Teaching in the mother tongue is also a means of stabilizing the child's personality and of offering ethnic and linguistic minorities the opportunity of receiving an education in the mother-tongue language within the national school system. Some receiving countries (namely the Netherlands and Sweden) have adopted a multicultural educational policy favouring education in the mother tongue. Wider recognition of such a policy would be the right approach to the question of the education of immigrant children.

In order for the whole educational system to be successful in providing children of migrant workers with truly bicultural tuition, efforts should be intensified to improve the education of migrant children in three major areas: introductory teaching, mother-tongue instruction and teacher training.

With regard to vocational training, all available data reveal that young migrants are under-represented in the vocational training courses offered in most European receiving countries and are over-represented in courses that lead to semi-skilled jobs. A recent OECD study on the employment of young migrants in Europe shows that the great majority of employed migrants under 25 years of age are manual workers, including apprentices: 70 per cent in Sweden; more than 75 per cent in Belgium; and nearly 85 per cent in France and the Federal Republic of Germany. The breakdown by sex shows that this proportion reaches 90 per cent for adolescent males in France and the Federal Republic of Germany. 60/

The major reasons why migrant children find themselves severely handicapped as far as their occupational future is concerned are: the deficiencies in the education system, the low socio-economic status of migrant children and the lack of facilities for vocational guidance and training to meet the specific needs of migrants. The study specifically draws conclusions on the inferior situation of second-generation migrants before and after their entry into working life. During the schooling and the subsequent training on which their occupational future depends, language is always an obstacle for migrants, from asking for guidance to approaching the authorities in search of a job. Opportunities for access to the public education and training system, which is open to both nationals and foreigners, are apt to remain theoretical or to concern only a small number of young migrants unless specific actions are taken.

The low level of education and the lack of vocational training have put young migrants at a disadvantage when entering the labour market. All data on the employment of young foreigners in Europe lead to the conclusion that, in the current economic crisis, they are much more vulnerable to unemployment than national youth. In the Federal Republic of Germany, for example, in the period between September 1978 and September 1980, unemployment among young foreigners under 25 years of age rose by 10.1 per cent while the number of unemployed nationals in the same age group decreased by 11.4 per cent. According to the latest SOPEMI report, the situation continued to deteriorate between September 1980 and April 1981: unemployment among all foreign workers in this period rose from 4.8 to 7.1 per cent. In France, the total number of unemployed increased by more than 50 per cent between March 1978 and March 1981, while among the young foreigners under 25 years of age, there was an 88.7 per cent increase in unemployment. In Sweden in 1980, the unemployment rate for young foreigners between the ages of 20 and 24 was 6.4 per cent, compared with 3.7 per cent for the total active population. 61/

Concerned about the current trends, nearly all the receiving countries have for several years been developing occupational guidance and training schemes for young people leaving school with no qualifications and little chance of finding a job. A common feature of the schemes has been the effort to achieve the social and occupational integration of these young people. Along with "traditional" courses designed to compensate for an inadequate general education, numerous socio-pedagogical and psychological assistance schemes have been introduced.

The examples given below describe the main directions recent important developments are taking:

(a) In France and Norway, efforts are being directed towards increasing the capacity of the legislative machinery, which is accessible to nationals and foreigners alike, making it flexible enough not to exclude the most underprivileged of the young;

(b) In the Federal Republic of Germany, a programme for the vocational training and social integration of the young has enjoyed notable success: from 1979 to 1980 the number of places offered more than doubled, reaching 15,000 in 1980-1981, only to fall again (11,000 in the autumn of 1982) as a result of the decline in the reuniting of families;

(c) In Austria, special classes have helped more young foreigners to reach secondary level and thus gain admission to apprenticeship schemes combining factory training with theoretical instruction in vocational schools: in six years (1976-1982), the number of foreign apprentices quadrupled;

(d) In Denmark, the rules for the admission of foreigners to basic occupational training courses were amended in 1982 in order to put foreigners on the same footing as Danes. Moreover, lessons in the mother tongue are offered and the possibility of bringing in bilingual teachers is under consideration;

(e) In the Netherlands, the final version of the memorandum concerning minorities was published in 1982 in the form of a preliminary discussion paper. It dealt with the problems of the second generation in detail and proposed a number of measures to improve their chances of success in education and employment. 62/

2. Specific problems of migrant women

The situation of women in the major receiving countries of Europe has been given increasing attention during the last decade, the main reason being the growing proportion and role of women in the migrant population, as well as the feminization of the foreign labour force (as shown in chapter I).

In the European receiving countries, in general, most legislation on women's rights does not discriminate in any way against female migrants. But, like all foreigners, migrant women in several countries encounter legal barriers in their access to and mobility within the labour market. Moreover, access to the labour market and restrictions on mobility are generally more severe for women than for men, and some restrictions have increased in recent years. In many countries, the issue of work permits to newly arriving wives of migrant workers depends on how long their husbands have spent in the country and the current employment situation.

In France, up to 1981, it was standard administrative practice to refuse a work permit, where legally possible, to any migrant woman and to limit the issuance of residence permits. In 1981 labour market restrictions were lifted for all women entering the country for family reunification. In the Federal Republic of Germany, in 1979, a waiting period of 2-4 years was introduced: although newly arrived wives could be refused access to the labour market on the basis of the employment situation, they could be granted a work permit after the waiting period had elapsed, depending on their nationality and the industry concerned. In practice, they were allowed access only to industries that were particularly short of labour. By 1982, 77.6 per cent of the migrants needing a work permit were in possession of one that generally gave unrestricted access. Later, wives entering after 1984 were wholly barred from the labour market. 63/

In some cases, migrant women may suffer direct discrimination because of nationality or sex, irrespective of their educational level, skills or legal status. Whereas in less attractive sectors, especially industry, migrant women are making their way into traditionally "male" jobs and training courses, they can encounter racist and sexist obstacles in the more attractive parts of the tertiary sector regardless of their qualifications.

Despite the serious obstacles encountered by migrant women in the labour market, they have continued to enter it in one way or another. As some studies conclude, the tightening of restrictions has had the effect of boosting domestic service and increasing undeclared employment. 64/

Occupational patterns of migrant women vary according to the conditions in each country and the structure of the labour market. Migrant women often hold the least prestigious and most poorly paid jobs, many in branches of the economy where competition is fierce, such as the textile and garment industries, which have been deserted by national women. However, more migrant women than national women work in industrial occupations because in industries dominated by male workers, migrant women are offered quite good wages. A large percentage of migrant women are public employees, particularly in public health.

Occupational areas of female employment that deserve particular attention are domestic work, heavy industrial work, and work on sub-contracts and in family enterprises. The conditions of domestic workers sometimes are claimed not to have changed significantly during the last century. It is particularly difficult to enforce better working conditions for domestic workers because of the dependent relationship between the employer and the employee and also because women who are likely to work in private households have poor knowledge of the language of the host country. For many migrant women, work on sub-contracts means many hours of work for poor pay. An advantage, as perceived by the worker, is that the work takes place at home, which lessens the need for special child-care arrangements. Women working in family enterprises are also likely to perform many hours of work that certainly do not give them individually the economic reward offered by employment on the open market. Women in industry are particularly exposed to health hazards when they work in industrial environments that are designed mainly for male workers. The presence of many migrant women in heavy industry makes the adaptation of

industrial work for women a question of prime significance and, as the areas
of traditional employment for women contract under the impact of the current
economic crisis in Western Europe, the question will increase in importance.

Migrant women generally earn less than both migrant men and national
women. Women working in male-dominated industrial work, however, earn more
than national women, and women in certain service work also earn well because
they work exceptionally long hours. Migrant women, on the whole, work more
hours a week than national women do and it is not uncommon for migrant women
to have two or three jobs at the same time. This heavy work-load has been
documented for women from Greece and Yugoslavia.

Unemployment is more frequent among female migrants than among male
migrants because the educational and training levels of female migrants are
not high enough to help them to retrain for another job. At the same time,
they often have large families and this extra burden is too heavy to allow
them free time outside working hours for training or social participation.
Equal employment opportunities, therefore, do not really exist for these
migrant women, who usually manage to get only low-grade unskilled jobs. In
fact, they often fail to take full advantage of the rights they do have
because of lack of information, lack of training and lack of time and
motivation.

Non-working migrant women are sometimes treated as a particularly
disadvantaged group. They are often considered to live isolated lives, shut
up in the house all day in a strange and incomprehensible environment. Some
female migrants are isolated because of child-rearing responsibilities and,
unlike male migrants, may not at first have sufficient contacts with the
people of the host country to be able to pick up its language, customs,
standards and laws quickly and to grasp the arrangements for welfare and
medical services. Not speaking the language of the host country well enough,
they often cannot read newspapers, official notices and the instructions on
household products, and they often lack the necessary education and skills to
enter the labour market. Quite frequently, wives are forbidden any recreation
outside the home without the permission of their husbands. As a result, the
migrant woman gradually becomes alienated from her working husband and her
children, who quickly adapt themselves to the new linguistic and social
environment.

Because migrant women are not granted the same facilities as migrant men,
European host countries should put more emphasis on initiation programmes to
help the former to participate in the labour market and community life, and
should set up vocational training programmes for the different categories of
women to improve their employment prospects.

3. Social condition of migrants in the Middle East

The dramatic increase in the migrant labour force in the oil-producing
countries of the Middle East is a comparatively new phenomenon, the social
consequences of which have not so far been sufficiently covered by international studies. It seems reasonable, therefore, to make a more general
assessment of the social situation of migrant workers and their families on
the basis of the information available.

(a) Legal status

The legal status of migrants is affected by the policies of many of the
receiving countries, which do not view themselves as immigration countries.

They consider all migrant labour as transient. Their declared aim is to retain migrant labour until they develop their own manpower, regardless of the time needed to do so. In recent years, an increasing number of Governments have adopted stricter policies to control the flows of migrants and to limit the growth of migrant stocks. As shown above, there has been a growing preference for Asian manpower and for contractors who bring their workers with them, without encouraging them to remain. At the same time, there has been a stricter enforcement of regulations on residence and work permits.

All these policies have affected first of all the legal status of migrant workers. Receiving countries in the area covered by the Economic and Social Commission for Western Asia (ESCWA) do not grant the status of permanent residents to migrant workers, regardless of their skills, occupations or nationalities. A migrant's residence is completely dependent upon his or her holding a job continuously. Until 1983, residential visas were granted to workers in the public sector, which were valid for as long as the workers were employed in that sector. Now, a five-year residence permit is granted, provided the migrant holds his or her job. Migrants working for the private sector are usually granted one- or two-year residence permits, which are renewable upon request by employers.

The fact that migrant workers are not granted permanent residence contributes to the high degree of insecurity that they experience. The insecurity is less severe for government employees, since civil service jobs are of a long-term and stable nature. Usually government employees spend a much longer period of time in the region (10-20 years) than private sector employees (5 years). Migrants working for the private sector (including the domestic sector) experience a more tense feeling of insecurity owing to the "guarantee system" upheld in the labour-receiving countries. According to this system, the Government will grant a limited residence permit to a migrant worker only if he or she is guaranteed by a native citizen. The guaranteeship could be in the form of a personal (in the case of domestic labour) or a company guarantee. The guarantor has the power to terminate a migrant's residence by terminating his or her employment, in which case the migrant worker is asked to leave the country within 7 to 14 days. The migrant worker's residence could be continued on two conditions: (a) if the original guarantor agrees to transfer the guarantee to a new guarantor and (b) if the worker finds a guarantor before his or her deportation date. In the case of domestic labour (maids, cooks, gardeners, private drivers), the guarantor can ask for immediate deportation after having paid the worker's current wages. The guarantor is not required by law to stick to the initial oral or written terms of employment, and has only to pay the worker's fare back home.

Legally, migrant workers cannot own property or a business venture. However, they are usually allowed to be partners in a business, provided 51 per cent of the shares are registered in the name of a native citizen. Moreover, the restriction of business licences to native citizens has led to a wide-scale profit-making market whereby private citizens "sell" business licences to migrants in return for a fixed annual sum of money. This applies particularly to small businesses, such as groceries, laundries and workshops for automobile repairs.

Before 1980, migrant workers in the Middle East had a relatively high degree of freedom of movement between employment sectors and within sectors. All they needed was the consent of their employer or guarantor. Since 1980, receiving countries have introduced new measures that greatly restrict the freedom of movement of labour between sectors. Moving within the private sector is still possible but more difficult. Moving from the public to the private sector, or vice versa, is no longer possible; migrant workers wishing to do so have to leave the country for a period of 6-12 months before new work and residence permits can be issued to them. 65/

(b) Working conditions

Despite the adequacy of labour laws in the receiving countries, two problems weaken the laws significantly. First, they exclude a large number of workers, such as domestic workers, workers who graze and raise livestock, small shopkeepers employing fewer than five workers, unskilled or manual labourers, daily wage workers and seamen. Secondly, the laws are often violated by employers, a fact observed during a survey conducted by the Arab Planning Institute (API), Kuwait, in five labour-receiving countries in 1982. One labour official even said that contracts with unskilled and semi-skilled labourers were just a formality and that non-adherence to labour laws by employers was encouraged by the excessive supply of migrant manpower in the labour markets of immigration countries of the Middle East. The survey also showed that only about 2-10 per cent of Asian workers facing problems with their employers took their cases to court. 66/

Wages. Based on the information available the following conclusions may be drawn:

(a) First, there are often no minimum wages in the public or private sectors. Wages vary according to supply and demand and according to the bargaining power of individual workers. Wages could be as low as 20 Kuwaiti dinars a month for unskilled labourers and maids;

(b) Secondly, in two receiving countries of the Middle East (Kuwait and Oman), there is a dualistic wage scale for citizens and migrants, whereby citizens are paid higher wages and other benefits for doing the same work as migrants. This practice is justified as a means of redistributing national income to citizens. In the remaining countries there is only one scale of wages for citizens and migrants: both receive equal wages and equal benefits for the same jobs;

(c) Thirdly, wages are often based on bargaining power, which is tied to a migrant's home country and its standard of living. Employers, especially in the private sector, pay American and European workers more than they pay Arab workers, and pay Arab workers more than they pay Asian workers. The explanation for this practice is the fact that the employees accept working for less. Even within each broad national and geographical category there is a large wage differential. For instance, Egyptians are the worst paid among Arab workers on the pretext that their country has the lowest rate of wages and that that fact will make Egyptians willing to accept work for wages that are 30 per cent or even 50 per cent lower than those of a Lebanese or a Palestinian doing the same work. There is also a wage differential among Asians from various countries. For instance, the salary of a Filipino maid is double that of a maid from Sri Lanka: the salary of an Indian maid falls in between. The API survey referred to above found that unskilled Asian workers are paid almost half the wages of Arab workers. Pakistani workers are paid 1.5 times more than similar workers from Bangladesh or India. There is less variation in wages according to migrants' nationalities within the public than the private sector, and less among skilled, technical and professional workers than among unskilled and semi-skilled workers;

(d) Fourthly, evidence collected by the API survey showed that unskilled migrant workers were required to work up to 12 hours a day. Adherence to overtime payments was high in government projects and large private projects, but was low in small private projects. About 60 per cent of the Asian workers interviewed said that they worked only eight hours, while 40 per cent said that they worked more than eight hours (9 to 12 hours) daily without receiving additional pay. Finally, migrants who work in the domestic sector (maids, gardeners, guards, private chauffeurs etc.) are overworked. Often they work from early in the morning until bedtime. Some are deprived of their weekly holiday.

(c) Living conditions

Earlier, housing was not much of a problem in the region: the private sector was able to provide most migrant workers with adequate housing at a reasonable rent. The turning point occurred in 1976 when rents went up owing to a steep rise in land prices. Investors in real estate stopped building ordinary or average housing, and turned to investing in luxurious apartments where profits were higher at rents beyond the means of most migrant workers. Moreover, in 1977-1978 most governments in ESCWA receiving countries allowed landlords to double old rents and gave them the right to double rents every five years thereafter. In addition, many landlords started to remodel their old buildings. They demolished the old low-rent buildings and constructed luxurious high-rent buildings. These developments have put a heavy burden on most migrant workers.

There are two main types of housing available for migrant workers, blocks of flats and collective or group houses. Blocks of flats are more expensive and are usually occupied by migrant families or medium- to high-income bachelors who can afford such housing. Flats vary in quality from the relatively convenient to the very convenient, depending on the monthly rent. The second type of housing is generally of very poor quality, usually consisting of very old houses in the old city quarters that have been deserted by their owners because they are no longer considered fit to live in, or of old deserted public warehouses. The typical group house is composed of 8-10 rooms occupied by 100-120 single migrant workers. The majority of the workers residing in these houses are unskilled Asians (Indians, Pakistanis, Bangladeshis, followed by Egyptians).

(d) Education of children

In the ESCWA labour-receiving countries, the language of tuition in public schools and universities is mainly Arabic (except for medicine, engineering and science), which means that only Arab migrants are able to attend public schools. Private schools can be grouped in two broad categories: Arab, and non-Arab or foreign. Private Arab schools are owned mostly by nationals, or jointly by nationals and Arab migrants. The same is true of European schools (English, French). Asian (i.e. Indian, Iranian, Pakistani etc.) communities are allowed to open and run their own private schools.

In the 1950s and 1960s, the children of Arab migrants faced no problems in attending public schools where they would receive free education, free school uniforms and free meals. The situation, however, changed drastically in the 1970s and the 1980s owing to an enlarged student body. Restrictive measures and rules were set in order to limit the number of migrant children attending public schools.

(e) <u>Training</u>

Major labour-receiving countries in the Middle East have established
relatively modern, advanced and well-equipped training centres, such as teacher
training, public health, nursing, commercial, communications, industrial and
technological institutes. However, places at all these institutes are largely
restricted to nationals. Migrants can form only 10 per cent of the student
body, despite the fact that technical and vocational education in the region
is undesired by citizens and that such institutes operate far below their
capacity. The highly advanced technical and vocational regional training
centre at Qatar, for instance, which can train 2,200 students, has been
operating for several years at a capacity of only 700 trainees. 67/

(f) <u>Provisions made by the sending country for migrant workers abroad</u>

Major sending countries in Asia have made some provisions to protect and
to assist their labour migrants in foreign countries. Several countries have
appointed labour attachés to assist in settling the grievances of their
workers in foreign countries. In 1983, Bangladesh appointed labour attachés
in countries with more than 5,000 Bangladeshis. Pakistan has appointed
community welfare attachés in 17 host countries to settle disputes and to
promote the general welfare of workers. The Republic of Korea has labour
attachés in Iraq, Jordan, Kuwait, the Libyan Arab Jamahiriya, Qatar, Saudi
Arabia and the United Arab Emirates. The Government also requires employers
to have a labour administration organization at each work place, as well as a
labour management council and a grievance handling office.

Labour attachés have multiple responsibilities, including the promotion
of labour migration, and they do not have sufficient time to handle all the
problems that arise. In addition, they cannot systematically check all work
sites to detect poor working and living conditions and to unearth violations
of labour contracts. They are usually reduced merely to responding to serious
complaints and conducting occasional spot checks of work places. Moreover,
the sending countries are often pro-employer in dealing with labour relations,
so the labour attachés are rarely advocates for the rights of workers.

Almost all Asian sending countries have minimum standards for employment
contracts. Some countries have developed model employment contracts and other
countries require that all employment contracts should be reviewed by government officials. Standard terms of contracts deal with such matters as wages,
hours of work, accommodation, food, transportation, vacation, home leave,
medical care, worker safety and health, and compensation for accidents.
Government regulations are sometimes very detailed on these matters. For
example, the Republic of Korea has stipulated that companies employing its
nationals overseas must follow regulations for worker accommodation regarding
the minimum ceiling height, the type of toilet and bathing facilities and even
the number of table tennis tables and other recreational facilities available.

A few Asian countries have established welfare funds to provide services
to migrant workers abroad. In the Philippines, both the recruitment agencies
and the overseas contract workers are required to contribute to a workers'
welfare fund. In Pakistan, the Overseas Pakistani Foundation provides social
benefits and welfare assistance to migrant workers and their families at home
and abroad. Each worker leaving on a foreign assignment pays 500 Pakistan
rupees as part of the fee for clearance by the Protector of Emigration. The
Philippine Government has established a Regional Labour Centre for the Middle
East, which is responsible for promoting the welfare of migrant workers.

4. Schooling of children in other regions

With regard to the schooling of children in Africa, the situation differs from country to country; as a rule both national and migrants' children are registered at compulsory schools, where they exist. However, problems arise where migrants are concentrated in one place. It is not certain that the Governments of receiving countries will build more schools to accommodate migrants' children, if such schools were not foreseen when other schools were being planned and built. Not many studies are available, but it can be expected that even if migrant children have more opportunities for education in the immigration country than in their own country, they are less fortunate than nationals who will, because of their social network, obtain places in school more easily. 68/ If the schooling has to be paid for, migrants' children may be at a disadvantage because their parents may be too poor to pay the fees owing to the precarious financial situation of migrants.

In Latin America, children of migrant workers have the same access to education at all levels as children of the receiving country. The absence of significant language differences in Latin American countries makes the educational integration of migrant children easier. However, since school systems are not designed for the children of migrants, such children may run the risk of being isolated because they are unfamiliar with the culture of the country of origin; they may even be given an adverse image of that culture. In their eagerness to communicate, children may reject the culture of their parents and adopt that of the receiving society, which may estrange children from parents.

Another problem facing migrant children is that of recognition of the equivalence of certificates of education obtained in the country of origin. At the Latin American regional seminar on Latin American migrations and their effects on children, wives and families, held at Caracas in 1980, a recommendation was put forward, demonstrating the existing deficiencies in the following terms:

"That admission to the school system at the appropriate level according to the years of study completed and approved in the country of origin should be facilitated for migrant minors, who should be given time to produce the statutory certificates and to take any missing subjects. If they lack the statutory certificates, they should be subject to an appraisal."

5. Maintenance of cultural and national identity

One of the most pronounced problems migrant workers and their families face is cultural and national identity, which is particularly critical at the time when adolescence begins. In many receiving countries, the cultural identity of second-generation migrants is formed under conditions of conflict. On the one hand, the school, the mass media, life-styles and many other factors induce young migrants to adopt the culture of the host country. On the other hand, the language barrier and discrimination at school and in society contribute to the marginality of the second generation. This marginality, as well as the cultural influence of the family, keeps the culture of their country of origin (language, traditions, forms of social life) present as a reality in the host country.

Some social scientists believe that only contact with both cultures, or rather cultural pluralism, will enable young foreigners to choose the culture that suits them best or to identify with elements from the cultural expression and languages of both countries. In any case, it is extremely important that both the receiving country and the country of origin provide young migrants with all possible assistance in the preservation and propagation of the culture of the country of origin.

In European receiving countries, various programmes are being implemented by governmental bodies and private organizations, in co-operation with the countries of origin, to help migrants preserve their national culture. In France, for example, associations of migrants receive subsidies from the Fonds d'Action sociale for various types of activities designed to promote expression of the home culture. Some sending countries (Morocco, Portugal and Senegal) regularly arrange drama tours. Radio and television programmes in the migrants' mother tongue are produced. In addition, sending countries supply municipal libraries and local associations with books and magazines in the sending country's language. In the Federal Republic of Germany, local radio stations broadcast daily 40-minute programmes prepared by the Turkish Radio and Television Association; there is also a weekly television programme in Turkish. The major Turkish newspapers are available for the immigrant community. In several regions of the country, Turkish cultural centres have been established. In Sweden, the Government contributes to the production of literature in foreign languages and also provides public libraries with funds for purchasing literature from sending countries.

Various services in receiving countries have been established by the countries of origin. In the Federal Republic of Germany, Greece has established several facilities, such as the Greek Orthodox Church, the International Meeting House, the Department of Foreign Residence and the Youth Service, which provide social welfare and cultural services for foreign children. Yugoslavia gives considerable attention to the preservation of the cultural and national identity of its nationals working abroad through its active support to migrants' clubs and associations. There are an estimated 900 associations of Yugoslav citizens in Europe. Yugoslavia has established seven cultural and information centres in Western European receiving countries, as well as various delegations to help migrant workers and their families in solving their many problems in maintaining cultural links with the country of origin. Links are also maintained with the country of origin through the organization of travel to the country of origin; in 1980 alone, about 3,500 migrant workers' children visited Yugoslavia, and the number was doubled in 1981. Italy, Spain and some other countries have set up cultural and information centres that broadcast special radio and television programmes in collaboration with national broadcasting corporations and video centres. The cultural centres also distribute local newspapers, magazines, books and brochures, and organize national and religious holidays or festivals and visits by travelling theatre groups or exhibitions.

In intra-African migration, no public institutions deal specially with the problem of preserving migrant culture and of helping migrants to maintain links with the country of origin. In the receiving countries, there are a multitude of cultures and at the national level, the desire is often to amalgamate all the different cultures of the country and to create a national culture, thus minimizing friction between ethnic groups. Often a kind of general culture, drawn from the various societies of the region, is preserved to check the pervading influence of Western culture.

Special programmes on television, and radio broadcasts in the migrants' languages, can be found in some countries. In Côte d'Ivoire, Ghana, Nigeria and Senegal, programmes feature news and cultural events in the languages of the migrants. In many instances, because of shared languages in receiving and

sending countries, the migrants also benefit from programmes given in these
languages. For example, Yoruba is spoken in Niger and Nigeria; Diula is
spoken in Burkina Faso, Côte d'Ivoire, Guinea and Mali; Swahili is spoken in
several East African countries. Côte d'Ivoire is a country where programmes
are directed perhaps to a specific group of migrants. Although Moré is not
the native language of Côte d'Ivoire, it is the language spoken by the
majority of migrants from Burkina Faso. Programmes on television and radio
are broadcast in Moré because of the relative importance of this group of
migrants (50 per cent of all migrants) in Côte d'Ivoire. Assistance to
migrants' associations, cultural or sports societies is found mostly at the
private level. Migrants have associations that, _inter alia_, organize social
events to keep alive their cultural heritage and to keep migrants, especially
children, in touch with their beliefs and customs.

No systematic effort is made in the Latin American countries to maintain
the links of emigrants and their families with the country of origin. On the
contrary, disapproval is usually shown when the various groups celebrate their
countries' independence days, because this custom is assumed to be a symptom
of non-integration into the host country. As a rule, the only recognition of
the immigrants' culture consists of celebrations at which migrants wear their
national dress, perform national dances and songs or serve national dishes.
The most widespread expression of the migrants' cultural identity is the
organization of community associations. However, such associations do not
receive official support in carrying out their activities; as a rule they have
to rely on members' subscriptions. Religious organizations also help migrants
to preserve their culture. The group of Roman Catholic institutions of the
countries in the north of the South American continent maintain a socio-
cultural programme, whose purpose is to promote interchange among different
national groups and to bring them closer to each another. Activities under
the programme concentrate on such aspects as folklore, handicrafts, cuisine,
recreation and other forms of artistic and cultural expression. Migrant
families are thus helped to preserve their national and cultural identity, and
thereby enrich the culture of the host country.

6. Social isolation

It should be noted that despite the fact that a number of measures have
been tried by receiving countries in recent years to facilitate the social
integration of migrant populations, these measures have not led to any
noticeable progress. _De facto_ social isolation is a reality of everyday life
for migrant workers and their families and is conditioned by the interplay of
economic, cultural and social aspects of the problems posed and experienced by
foreign workers. As a recent report by the Council of Europe notes:

"Low pay and difficulty in effectively communicating with the local
population leads to their occupying very cheap slum accommodation and
choosing public meeting places (bars, squares, stations) where groups of
the same race tend to gather. These turn into ghettos where extreme
poverty leads to despair and crime." 69/

For children of migrant workers, education in the host country ought to
be instrumental in bridging the gap between them and the local population.
However, as indicated above, this is not always the case. Owing to their
cultural environment and their poor knowledge of the host country's main
language, the children of migrant workers often have great difficulty in
adapting. If the teachers devote the necessary amount of time to these
children, they are accused of holding up the normal progress of the class as
a whole, and schools with high percentages of foreign pupils are accordingly

deserted by the local children. This leads to the isolation of migrant
children at school. In many receiving countries, disparities between the
situations of national and foreign pupils in education persist.

The situation of migrant populations is further aggravated by a growing
intolerance of the presence of migrant workers in the major receiving countries.
In Switzerland, a government bill advocating the consolidation of the acquired
rights of migrant workers, which was submitted to a referendum of 6 June 1982,
was rejected. In France, as <u>The Economist</u> reports, "racial tension boils up"
while some politicians attack migrants as welfare scroungers, creators of
unemployment and a menace to social peace. 70/ Hostility towards foreigners
has led in some places to violence. There have been street battles in Brixton,
near London and Liverpool. In Belgium, France and the Federal Republic of
Germany, cases of violent attacks on migrant workers have been reported.

Concerned with the outbursts of xenophobia in various European countries,
the Council of Europe has emphasized the need to strengthen the role of public
authorities in combating this problem, as well as to implement the rights of
migrants, as granted in international instruments, particularly with regard to
accommodation, schooling, occupational and linguistic training, teaching of
the mother tongue, working conditions, social security and social welfare.
Such measures would make it possible to avoid the dramatic consequences of
maladjustment and rootlessness. The need to launch a campaign to make the
public aware of the problem has also been stressed. This campaign should be
conducted by the public authorities with the collaboration of all associations
concerned, and also by the mass media. 71/

7. Undocumented migrants

Illegal migration is a phenomenon that has recently become important
because it concerns many developing, as well as industrialized, countries in
all parts of the world. It is clear from available estimates that the
phenomenon affects a large number of persons, ranging from the foreigner who
works in another country without complying with legal requirements to the rest
of the work-force in that country, as well as clandestine intermediaries and
employers and the Governments involved.

In most cases, organizations illegally recruit and transport workers to
another country after arranging for them a contract of employment, which is
very often false, under which they will receive wages far higher than those
that they are earning in their own country. Frequently, the workers concerned
are foreigners who enter the country as tourists and, after finding employment,
remain there without regularizing their situation. In other cases, the persons
concerned, whether because of a lack of information or simply because of their
urgent need for work, leave their country without waiting to be issued with the
necessary papers and with no more than a hope of finding a job. Finally,
refugees who, between the time they reach the country of asylum and the time
they acquire the status of refugees, lack the necessary documents, may also be
regarded as migrants in an irregular situation.

The situation resulting from unauthorized migration is distressing for
the workers themselves and especially for their families. Migrant workers in
an irregular situation as a rule:

(a) Receive lower wages than workers in a legal situation;

(b) Have no social security coverage;

(c) Cannot apply to any official body (trade union, labour court etc.), in the event of any claim concerning labour matters, precisely because they are in breach of the law;

(d) Perform unhealthy or dangerous work without adequate protection or safety;

(e) Might be treated as virtual criminals and are obliged to live in very poor conditions, both with regard to housing and integration into society;

(f) Frequently live apart from their families; reunification is very difficult and has to be achieved, if at all, by illegal methods. Consequently, the education of children will also be affected by this irregular situation.

The presence of migrants in an irregular situation represents a problem for the receiving country. Difficulties of detecting such workers make it impossible for the Government to plan for or to know the real situation on the labour market. It also leads to bad feelings on the part of legally employed workers who do the same kind of job or who are unemployed. Frequently, they come to blame the unauthorized workers for their own lack of employment. Often the Government of the receiving country itself reinforces feelings of xenophobia and discrimination among its nationals towards unauthorized workers, in an attempt to explain a high level of unemployment.

Expulsion is currently one of the main measures regarding illegal migrants that have been introduced into the legislation of many States. It may be regarded as an adequate protective or precautionary measure for a receiving country in relation to a foreigner, but it is an extreme one that should have its limits, namely, that the foreigner concerned should be allowed to apply to the courts to contest a deportation order given by the competent authorities. However, the legislation of many countries makes it impossible or extremely difficult to resort or to appeal to the courts against a deportation order, thus violating one of the principal human rights.

The main reason why foreigners in an irregular situation are being expelled with increasing frequency is the extreme situation being provoked by the recent excessive rise in the number of unauthorized migrants and their very poor living and working conditions. The dramatic mass expulsion of migrants from Nigeria early in 1983 is the most recent example of the application of such measures. Under a new order, unskilled workers, street vendors and unemployed persons were required to leave the country immediately; skilled workers were given a month to do so; professionals were allowed to stay permanently once their employers had obtained the necessary permits.

Regrettably, this is not the first instance of such an extreme situation. Over the last decade, thousands of Nigerians have been similarly expelled from various African countries (Ghana, the Sudan, Zaire etc.).

Many countries have recently revised their immigration laws in order to maximize their control over foreigners in an irregular situation. In all such laws, the changes relate essentially to deportation, on the one hand, and regularization on the other. However, in many countries, regularization of the situation of workers in breach of the law involves requirements with which it is extremely difficult for most unauthorized workers to comply.

To alleviate the harmful effects of illegal migration, a number of measures have been recommended by the international organizations concerned. For example, the Council of Europe, in its resolution (78) 44 on clandestine migration and the illegal employment of foreign workers:

(a) Recommended the adoption of preventive measures designed to eliminate misleading publicity, which might induce someone to become an illegal migrant, and to promote international co-operation to dismantle the networks of traffickers and intermediaries for this type of labour;

(b) Laid down a series of control measures to be taken by the countries of destination with a view to ensuring that the conditions governing migrant workers' residence and employment were complied with, at the same time ensuring close co-operation between national administrative authorities in the matter of the exchange and co-ordination of information;

(c) Recommended that Governments should ensure that national legislation laid down severe penalties for intermediaries and employers who engaged in or promoted the illegal employment of foreign labour;

(d) Recommended that repatriation should be considered as one of the means of controlling unlawful migration and employment, that the practical problems arising in that connection should be settled and that international agreements should be concluded where necessary. The resolution also stipulated that the rights that such workers had acquired in the course of their work in the matter of remuneration, social security and other benefits should be respected and that they should receive legal aid where it was needed to defend those rights.

D. Return to and reintegration into the country of origin

1. Bilateral co-operation

In recent years, wider recognition by some sending and receiving countries of their common interest in solving problems concerning the reintegration of returning migrants has led to the conclusion of bilateral agreements stipulating joint actions in this field.

According to an agreement between the Federal Republic of Germany and Turkey, a vocational training programme has been started to prepare Turkish workers to manage their own enterprises upon their return to Turkey. Under this agreement, a special fund has been established to extend credit to investment projects of migrants who have returned to Turkey. The Government of the Federal Republic of Germany is obliged to ensure the transfer of technology, consultancy and assistance in production and in running the migrants' industrial plants. The Turkish Government is obligated to grant customs and other benefits to those importing equipment for these plants. Since 1972, some 60 million deutsche mark were made available for direct incentives for the reintegration of Turkish workers, which were granted in the form of counselling, planning aids and further training, as well as for loans, interest and administrative expenses. Workers' companies currently run 140 firms in different branches. Bearing in mind secondary and tertiary effects, it is estimated that 34,000 jobs were created. So far, about 2,400 Turks returning from the Federal Republic of Germany have found employment in this way. 72/ The Federal Government recently decided to give financial incentives to increase the willingness of foreigners to return to their home countries.

Under an agreement signed in 1980 between Algeria and France on the return of migrants, the Government of France is obligated to pay a compensation equal to the average wage for four months to each returnee to Algeria who has worked in France for at least six months before applying for such compensation, and to pay the travel expenses of the returning workers and their dependants. The

Government of Algeria is obliged to continue and, if necessary, to reinforce the policy of customs and tax benefits for returnees and make it easier for them to solve their housing problems with the financial support of the French Government.

In Yugoslavia, a special fund for financing increased employment in economically underdeveloped and emigration regions was set up in 1978 with the aim of selecting the investment programmes to be financed and implemented jointly by Yugoslavia and countries receiving Yugoslav workers. Within the framework of the activities of the Fund so far, the Government of the Netherlands has granted financial assistance of 6 million Netherlands guilders for the implementation of two investment projects in Yugoslavia. In 1980-1981, the Fund selected more than 50 projects to be carried out in underdeveloped and emigration regions of Yugoslavia, and since then it has been making great efforts to ensure co-operation with the receiving countries in implementing these projects. 73/

Some initial efforts have been made to develop international co-operation in working out and implementing programmes for the successful return and reintegration of migrants. OECD has undertaken research to assess the experiences of individual countries of origin in attracting and utilizing migrants' savings, as well as on the nature and scope of services for the reintegration of migrants. An OECD project entitled "Experimental schemes for employment creation in high emigration regions" is designed to identify the possibilities for bilateral co-operation in migrant reintegration into the country of origin. The Council of Europe has carried out intensive research and activities designed to improve the education and social position of young migrants. In addition, the Council provides financial assistance to countries of origin in implementing reintegration schemes through its Resettlement Fund.

2. Unilateral measures by receiving countries

Some of the measures that were unilaterally introduced by several receiving countries, such as individual financial assistance to migrant workers who voluntarily return to the country of origin, soft credits for returning migrants to implement specific projects in the country of origin and schemes for vocational re-training of migrants, have been successful. Only a comparatively small number of migrants have been able to benefit from such forms of assistance, and migrant workers in general are reluctant to accept such aid because for them it means replacing the uncertainty of migration with the even greater uncertainty of return.

France and the Federal Republic of Germany, for instance, have introduced financial incentives to encourage migrant workers and their families to return to the country of origin. The bonus granted is generally financed by the capitalization of unemployment and family contributions, the reimbursement of social security contributions, public aids and aids to enterprises. The granting of a bonus is subject to compliance with a number of requirements. For instance, in France, workers qualify for these bonuses only if they are unemployed because they have been laid off. In the Federal Republic of Germany, such grants are made to migrant workers only if they are unemployed because the enterprise in which they have been working has gone bankrupt or has closed down, or if they have been working part time for a certain period.

However, as a recent report of the Council of Europe concludes, these measures have not been as successful as the Governments of France and the Federal Republic of Germany had hoped. Only those who had already decided to return home have availed themselves of the financial incentives offered. 74/

The reason for the lack of success is that, in times of crisis, workers remain where the prospects of finding jobs are better. It is therefore obvious that measures to promote a return to the country of origin, even if they are directed at a small and specific group, as in this case, do not make much sense if they are adopted only unilaterally.

3. Measures taken by sending countries

In most cases, in contrast to the emigration flows of earlier years, in which for the most part there was organized co-operation between the receiving and sending countries, there has been practically no co-operation between sending and receiving countries in the return of migrants. Workers frequently return because they have to, not because they want to. Many have failed in what they set out to do when they went to work abroad, so they return to their country of origin with few means or no means at all to facilitate their resettlement. In addition, as is commonly believed, returning migrants place an extra strain on the overall employment possibilities in their countries of origin and call for additional financial efforts there to create new working places under circumstances marked by an already high and growing unemployment rate.

In most countries of origin, the social welfare and economic provisions are often not available to facilitate the return of migrants and their social and occupational reintegration. The need for policies and programmes for the return and reintegration of migrants has been recognized by only a few sending countries. In Algeria, governmental bodies carry out a wide range of activities including: obtaining accurate information on employment requirements to be met by returning nationals; seeking employment opportunities for workers who would like to return; preparing short- and medium-term plans for the return of migrants; encouraging the recruitment of migrant workers; concluding agreements with employers; and issuing the visas required. In Tunisia, a special service has been established that, among other things, deals with: the occupational reintegration of returning migrants through job placement or as self-employed promoters of economic projects; housing; and other problems connected with resettlement of returning nationals. In Italy, Portugal and Spain, national, regional and local public, private and State institutions have set up emigration offices, legal and administrative services, vocational guidance and information services to help workers who wish to return to their countries of origin.

In Spain, an organization of co-operative enterprises, has been set up with a view to securing economic and human support for migrants who wish to return home and who are willing to contribute a suitable sum of money and personal labour on joining the co-operative. A number of courses have been organized for Spanish migrant workers in major receiving countries so as to acquaint those wishing to return home with the co-operative movement in Spain. In Yugoslavia, a new law on the protection of citizens temporarily employed abroad has been introduced. According to this law, social institutions in the country are responsible for the social and occupational reintegration of migrants. 75/ One important point to note is that migrants returning to Yugoslavia are not put at a disadvantage in the competition for jobs there. Since one of the criteria for establishing priorities when employing people in Yugoslavia is the duration of their unemployment, and since the period of a migrant's stay abroad is considered as a period of unemployment, returnees can successfully compete with unemployed workers at home. In addition, qualifications gained abroad by migrants are taken into account by the enterprises on the same basis as qualifications of workers who change their place of work within the country. It is also within the competence of the enterprises employing returnees to acknowledge the period of work abroad when calculating entitlements to certain social benefits (i.e., longer vacations, priority in solving housing problems etc.).

Attempts are being made to encourage faster development of "small business" units. Migrants are encouraged to invest their savings in the flows of the economy. Small businesses offer scope for such investment, and also provide other citizens with employment opportunities. Another possibility is for migrant workers to invest their savings in agriculture, in co-operation with organizations (i.e. enterprises), with the purpose of satisfying common needs.

In Yugoslavia, migrants can also invest their fixed-term deposit savings in the public sector of the economy, in order to create jobs for themselves. The so-called contractual organizations of associated labour that have been established for returnees have at their disposal considerable means of production and resources. The General Small Business Association of Croatia and the Union of Associations of Independent Businessmen of Croatia have worked out a model that consists of a pooling of labour and resources between organizations of associated labour and their new workers that have returned from temporary employment abroad. A work organization (or the basic organization of associated labour) is prepared to create a job for a returnee, provided that the returnee will import the necessary equipment for the purposes of the work of the organization, pooling the equipment with the enterprise concerned. On the basis of a contract (entitled a "self-management agreement on pooling"), the work organization will repay the returnee the value of the invested resources in new dinars within a specific period of time. 76/

In compliance with the regulations in force and with a view to their own employment, returnees from work abroad, like all other Yugoslav citizens, may invest their own resources in the development of private agricultural holdings, or set up private shops where they can also employ a statutorily prescribed number of other workers. Individual farmers and craftsmen can associate to form co-operatives with a view to promoting their work and business or can enter into sub-contracting arrangements with the social sector.

On their own initiative and employing their own resources, one or more returnees may, as mutually agreed upon, set up small-scale and, as a rule, labour-intensive, enterprises, where they can also employ other workers, with no restrictions as to their number such as apply to private shops. These organizations, known as contractual organizations of associated labour, can be considered a transitional form of economic activity by the private and social sectors, so that under given circumstances they can also evolve into an organization of associated labour in the social sector.

In Turkey, initiatives and efforts have branched off in two main directions, public or private, depending on the type of ownership involved. With regard to the former, assistance is given in the development of existing rural farm co-operatives, with a view to encouraging their expansion by returning migrants, as well as that of corporations for joint investment that have been established by migrants themselves. The appointment of migrants as private entrepreneurs has also yielded results. Studies have shown that returning migrants are interested in this kind of investment because they keep their independence and are provided with credit on favourable terms.

Migrants who return to their rural holdings often make the mistake of investing their money in expensive equipment and agricultural machines that cannot be put to efficient use on small plots of land. Returnees therefore increasingly turn to the establishment of service centres, the service sector being the only one that provides some possibilities for employment, even if the capital invested is not substantial. However, migrants experience considerable competition owing to the existence of too many service units.

In Turkey, there are three different models of workers' companies:

(a) Workers' joint-stock companies, established on the understanding that all initiatives must be taken abroad and that primarily the savings of Turkish workers employed abroad must be used;

(b) Associated public joint-stock companies that accept migrants' savings (established on the initiative of the Government, and utilizing the capital of migrant workers);

(c) Agricultural development co-operatives established in Turkey (with government assistance) and utilizing the foreign exchange savings of migrant workers. In the post-recession period, interest in the above modes of investment has grown considerably.

Most sending countries have introduced legislation to facilitate the importation of equipment that workers require to continue their occupations in their countries of origin, as well as the importation of any furniture, electrical appliances for the home and other personal possessions that they acquired abroad. Various benefits have been introduced for returning migrants, such as preferential interest rates on long-term foreign currency investments and exemption from custom duties on imported goods and equipment.

Some sending countries have taken measures aimed at helping returning children to reintegrate into the educational system. In Algeria, such measures include priority enrolment of returning children in various educational establishments and boarding schools, priority in granting scholarships and exemption from tests in Arabic. In establishments of higher education, students are allowed to make a choice when enrolling in faculties, institutes etc.; only elementary-level Arabic is required, and scholarships are awarded automatically. In Greece, mother-tongue courses are organized during the school holidays for children and teenagers attending school in a foreign country. Special introductory classes for children returning to the home country have been set up. In secondary schools, special provisions can be made for students who have not passed regular exams to pass from one class to the next. Free vocational training is available for children aged between 15 and 20 years who are selected from applicants that have completed their compulsory training in another country. In Finland, children returning from Sweden are usually integrated into an equivalent class; in case of linguistic difficulty the same teaching programme is offered in Swedish, and Finnish is studied as a main subject. Six hours of special tuition is also provided each week for children returning from other countries. In Yugoslavia, no supplementary education is organized for returning children, but they are provided individually with the necessary assistance.

Measures aimed at helping returning migrants with reintegration problems have been rather limited, however. Most returning migrants and members of their families do not find any assistance when they come back after temporary employment abroad. In Africa, Asia and Latin America, in the case of the normal return of migrants, there is neither an institutional network to give vocational guidance or family counselling nor are there special arrangements for schooling. But in most cases, certificates of study earned abroad by migrants' children are recognized.

In Africa, only in the case of expulsion do returning migrants and their families receive some help from public institutions. In such cases, the resettlement schemes developed by the countries of origin depend on the number of returnees, on the financial capability of the country, on the composition of the stream of migrants and on their willingness to accept help. Some countries just help the migrants for a few days and then let them find their own way in the country. Such help usually consists in providing food, clothing and shelter. Senegal has given financial aid, and land for farming has been offered also to people willing to settle in the rural zones. The Government often tries to have the savings and value of properties of the emigrants repatriated. A set of networks is usually created for a short time to provide counselling for the migrants and their families to help them integrate into their country's social and economic environment.

As the number of Asian migrant workers returning from assignments abroad continues to increase, the problems that they face will become more evident. Pakistan has about 500,000 returned workers and an estimated 5 per cent of all households in Pakistan have at least one returnee. More than 100,000 workers from the Republic of Korea return home each year, although many accept new contracts abroad. Over 30,000 migrant workers return permanently to Bangladesh each year. These workers may experience problems of reintegration into the labour force and social readjustment, but the extent of such problems is not well known. Undoubtedly, problems will be more serious for those who have been away longer. In some cases, the worker's absence is so short that serious problems are unlikely to arise. For example, migrant workers from Fiji who go to New Zealand obtain work permits initially for a four-month period with an option of a two-month extension. When an assignment is over, the worker is required to return to Fiji for twelve months before re-entering New Zealand. Problems are expected to be more acute when workers spend several years abroad, as in the case of returnees to Pakistan.

The emergence of problems among returning workers also depends on the plans of migrant workers when they complete their overseas contracts and whether or not they are able to fulfil their expectations upon their return. There is some evidence that returned workers often do not follow their original plans. In Pakistan, 63 per cent of the migrant workers said that they expected to start a business when they returned, but only 6 per cent of the returnees have actually started a business. 77/ An even higher percentage (77 per cent) of Filipino migrant workers expect to start a business upon their return, but it is unlikely that this goal will be attained by such a large proportion of returnees.

Workers who have been earning abroad several times the amount of pay they can reasonably expect to earn in their home countries may return home with unrealistically high job expectations. If unfulfilled, these expectations could be a potential source of social and political unrest. Most returning workers are able to find acceptable employment without much difficulty, however. In Pakistan, half of the returning workers reportedly found jobs immediately upon their return and an additional one third eventually found work. 77/ Two thirds of the returning Pakistani workers said that they did not have any adjustment problems when they returned, 26 per cent said that they had minor problems, and only 5 per cent complained of serious problems. Although the percentage of returnees facing serious problems was small, if this percentage were to be applied to all returnees, it would amount to about 25,000 persons. In the Philippines, 26 per cent of the migrant workers said that they thought it would be difficult for them to find a job when they returned to the Philippines, but no information is available on the actual difficulties of returnees. Measures taken so far to help returning migrants have been limited to the setting up of an assistance centre at Manila International Airport (to receive returning overseas contract workers, but this centre primarily deals only with immediate needs) and to the preferential treatment in housing given to returned migrants by the Government. According to Government policy, 10 per cent of all new flats must be sold first to returning overseas workers or to veterans receiving relief.

In Latin America, the only measure taken to assist and guide migrants on their outward and return journeys has been the establishment of frontier offices (in Colombia and Ecuador) in accordance with the Andean Instrument of Labour Migration. In Colombia, a reception centre has been set up under the National Social Pastoral Secretariat for Colombians deported from Venezuela. This centre deals with the reception, board and lodging of returnees, processes documentation, provides medical services and medicine, finds jobs and offers information and general guidance. It also holds periodic information meetings, runs educational campaigns at individual and group levels, and co-ordinates its activities with private and public bodies. In practice, however, the standards of operation and efficiency prescribed in the Instrument have not been attained.

It should be stressed that sending countries have had little influence on the level and pace of return migration, which has been largely based on the decisions of individuals and the policies of the receiving countries rather than on the need and desire of the sending countries.

From the experience of some sending countries, one general conclusion might be drawn: if measures designed to integrate returnees economically, socially and culturally into their country of origin are to be effective, they should be conceived as integral parts of plans for local and regional development and should envisage provisions for adequate employment for returnees, the productive utilization of migrants' savings and co-operation with the receiving countries in implementing reintegration schemes. In more general terms, the economic and social reintegration of migrants should be viewed as an integral part of the migratory policy of the country of origin, aimed at accelerating the development of underdeveloped regions and thus eliminating one of the main causes for the migration of the population.

If, however, the decision of migrants to return home is to be taken freely and independently, it is essential that bilateral and multilateral co-operation should be developed and intensified so that a better economic balance between immigration and emigration countries is achieved. Efforts should be made to correct a number of imbalances by adopting short- and medium-term solutions. Steps might be taken in the following directions:

(a) Creation of specific projects in the most backward regions of the countries of origin, financed out of the savings of migrant workers, by the receiving and sending countries;

(b) Location of jobs in the country of origin and adequate training for returning migrants. Public administration in both receiving and sending countries should create an information service on employment opportunities able to match supply and demand. The information should be as comprehensive as possible and cover employment possibilities, salary conditions, cost of living, housing available, education of children, transfer of social security rights, vocational training, utilization of savings etc.;

(c) Implementation of measures to help migrant children in adjusting to school systems in the country of origin;

(d) Efforts to encourage the competent authorities in the countries of origin to recognize secondary-education certificates and diplomas qualifying their holders for access to higher education, as well as professional qualifications and experience acquired abroad;

(e) As an essential step, the devising of measures to ensure that social rights acquired abroad are maintained after migrants have returned home, even in the absence of bilateral agreements. This means advocating that all the countries involved in contemporary migration should sign and become parties to a multilateral agreement.

III. CONCLUDING REMARKS

Despite the fact that international migration trends and policies have been changing rapidly in recent years, there is no indication that migration is diminishing in its importance as one of the appreciable factors of the world economy, politics and social life. As a recent United Nations survey on international migration policies and programmes states:

"While countries are not likely to bring about a halt in future migration neither are they likely to increase their intake dramatically. Rather, they will continue to fine tune immigration decisions, weighting humanitarian concerns against other political and social objectives, most likely by means of increasingly precise selection processes involving quotas, numerical weightings and so forth." 78/

Therefore, it is reasonable to assume that international migration will remain an economic, social and political issue with ramifications extended to many parts of the world; currently there are few countries that are not touched, in one way or another, by movements of migrant workers. The need for long-term comprehensive social welfare and related policies, in contrast to shorter-term objectives of a remedial nature that often turn out to be too late and too little, should be re-emphasized.

Some of the social problems stemming from the international migration of labour are of a long-standing character. They are: the unequal legal status of, and discriminatory practices against migrant workers and their families, the lack or inadequacy of social services provided for them by both sending and receiving countries, the difficulties in the reunification of families, the poor living conditions and the lack of assistance in case of eventual return to the country of origin. All these major characteristics of the social situation of migrant workers and their families are as valid today as ever, which is why any responsive social policy designed to improve the present position of migrants should give priority attention to their basic handicaps. At the international and regional levels, action should be taken to induce Governments to assume their commitments under existing international instruments, which represent the minimum required for the protection of migrant workers and their families. In addition, efforts should be made to revise and supplement existing conventions and agreements; the standard-setting and monitoring mechanisms evolved by ILO should be better utilized. The substantial progress made by the United Nations in the elaboration of an International Convention on the Protection of the Rights of All Migrant Workers and Their Families, pursuant to General Assembly resolution 34/172, is a positive development. It should be pointed out, however, that if the Convention is to contribute significantly to the improvement of the social position of migrant workers and their families, explicit provisions should be included with regard to family reunion, housing and other conditions for a normal family life, the education of children, health care and the preservation of the national and cultural identity of migrant workers, as well as minimum standards of services provided specifically for migrants in both sending and receiving countries. International co-operation at different levels should be further developed to ensure that the scope of social programmes on behalf of migrants is commensurate with the migrants' contribution to development.

New needs and dimensions arise, as a result of recent significant changes in world migration patterns, that have long-term implications for the social situation of migrant workers and their families.

By closing their frontiers for traditional labour migration in the early 1970s, some major receiving countries have perhaps reduced the flow of immigrant workers. But, as a result, the structure of the resident foreign population has been considerably modified. Consequently, the integration problems already encountered by immigrants are now assuming unprecedented proportions. Probably the most serious problem is that of the social integration of second-generation young migrants who account for a large and growing share of pupils in the receiving countries and who in the near future will form a substantial part of the work-force in those countries. Their current situation is described in recent research as rootless because young migrants feel foreign both in the countries of residence and in their parents' countries of origin. Mainly owing to their socio-economic and legal status in the countries of residence, young migrants find themselves at a disadvantage in such vitally important areas as education and training, and because of this, represent one of the most vulnerable groups with respect to unemployment. In view of the difficult economic situation prevailing in the major sending countries, it is unlikely that many second-generation young migrants will return to the countries of their parents' origin. However important the measures recently introduced in the countries of employment have been, they are too limited in scope to bring about a substantial improvement in the conditions for genuine integration of young migrants into the host society. Further and intensified efforts will be needed to improve the current unfavourable situation of migrant children and youths, particularly with respect to their education, vocational training and employment.

More attention should be given to the specific problems of migrant women. On the basis of the analysis of the patterns of migration to Western Europe, it is reasonable to conclude that the major European receiving countries will experience the continuation of female migration owing to family reunification, the growing tendency for women to emigrate independently and even illegally and the increasing participation of immigrant women in the labour force. Because migrant women are not granted the same facilities as migrant men, European host countries in particular should put more emphasis on initiation programmes to help migrant women participate in the labour market and community life and, above all, should set up vocational training programmes for the different categories of women to improve their employment prospects. However, the legal status of migrant women should not be solely dependent on their marital status; in case that changes, they should be awarded residence and work permits subject to the same conditions as immigrant men. Female migrants should have the same status as immigrant men if they are able to meet the residence and work permit requirements laid down by the immigration policy of the host country.

A lesson to be drawn from the experience of Western European receiving countries is that any comprehensive policy to improve the welfare of migrant workers should take into account the specific needs of their families and children, which does not mean separating the issue of the welfare of the migrant workers from that of the welfare of their families. Children derive not only their status, but also their social situation from their parents' condition. The first step in improving the situation of children might be to improve the situation of the parents, for instance by helping them to overcome their problems of adaptation to the host society and by improving their legal status and living conditions. Thus, any action taken to improve the situation of migrant workers with regard to recruitment, briefing, living and working conditions, social services, general education and vocational training and preparation for eventual return and reintegration would indirectly have a positive effect on the lives of migrant children and their families. At the same time, a number of issues directly affect the situation of children, such as pre-school education, schooling, vocational training and preservation of their national identity and culture. Obviously these issues should be fully taken into account in designing and implementing policies and programmes aimed at resolving the problems caused by labour migration.

A dramatic increase in foreign labour in the oil-producing countries of the Middle East, which has promoted project-tied and similar migration, also has serious social implications. Under the terms of this type of migration, virtually every aspect of the migrant workers' daily life is under the protection and control of the employer: they are forbidden to form unions while in the Middle East; minimum requirements for accommodation in the camps are not always met; the incidence of work-related deaths and injuries is high and on the increase; and the workmen's compensation system is unsatisfactory. In addition, issues of equal opportunity and treatment are unresolved. 79/ When workers arrive in the host country, the possibility of their being exploited is real. Instances in which workers' contracts were violated or even broken unilaterally by the employer have been reported in several countries. Physical and sexual abuse have also been reported, particularly in the case of female workers. There have been a number of reports in the press about the serious problems facing migrant workers' families in the major receiving countries of the region. 80/ Housing is a major problem for the majority of migrant workers and their families. The gap between wages and rents is growing fast, making adequate housing beyond the reach of migrant families. For example, in the case of newly built buildings, the average rents are higher than the average wages of most migrant workers. As a result, housing conditions of unskilled and semi-skilled migrant workers have deteriorated drastically. The general education needs of children of migrant workers are met with growing difficulty because of the rapidly increasing cost. Higher education and vocational training are practically inaccessible for most migrant children because they may only constitute 10 per cent of the total enrolment. A large segment of the migrant labour force faces enormous difficulties in family reunion. The fact that these problems have been neither studied nor discussed by the policy-makers at both ends of the migratory process gives rise for concern. More efforts at the national, regional and international levels will be needed to increase the awareness of the public and the Governments concerned of the social situation of the immigrant population and to seek solutions for the many social and humanitarian problems associated with migration.

At the other end of the migratory process to the Middle East, in the Asian sending countries, the recent massive emigration of labour also entails some social problems. One of the most pronounced of them is recruiting abuses. Although nearly all of the major labour-exporting countries already have laws to regulate recruitment, the enforcement of them needs to be improved. Governments also need to explore innovative ways of cutting the red tape that makes securing foreign employment an arduous and expensive process. As the number of returning Asian migrant workers increases, problems of reintegration and readjustment are likely to receive more attention. So far, most workers have not experienced serious problems after their return. Nevertheless, these workers have tangible needs in the areas of employment and investment and Asian Governments might consider expanding their employment services to take account of the special needs of returning labour migrants and develop investment schemes to channel the savings of migrant workers into more productive uses.

There is widespread concern that the present adverse economic conditions are contributing to the global increase in irregular migration and, consequently, are making migrants more vulnerable to exploitation, discrimination and abuses, including the neglect of their fundamental human rights. Irregular migration tends to inspire negative attitudes towards normal migration. In many parts of the world, there is a growing hostility on the part of the local population towards immigrants, who must live in a state of permanent insecurity, created by the uncertainty of their own and their children's social and occupational future. Unless properly managed, the situation may create unrest at the regional and international levels. Thus, more efforts should be made at the international, regional and local levels to improve the lot of migrant workers and their families and to search for solutions to their many problems based on a stronger interest in international co-operation and mutual development.

Much remains to be done to break the social barriers that characterize the situation of most migrant workers and their dependants. Improved methods of public information on the situation, needs and expectations of migrant children and their families, which could open up possibilities for enlarged social and political participation by migrant groups, would be desirable steps toward such a goal.

There is an apparent shortage of scientific data needed to understand all the social implications of contemporary labour migration. For example, research on the situation of children and families of migrant workers concentrates mainly on the Western European region, and there is little information on large parts of the world (Africa, Asia, Latin America). There is a general lack of information on the reintegration of migrant workers and their families into the country of origin. This shortage is disturbing, for it leads people to underestimate the difficulties that may be encountered when steps are taken to reduce the undesirable social effects of international migration. In this area, the United Nations and other organizations concerned have an essential role to play, particularly through research activities on the social consequences of migratory movements of workers in all regions of the world, and through meetings of experts to focus on the social implications of recent migratory trends. Further concerted efforts of the United Nations, ILO and other specialized agencies concerned will be needed to affirm the rights of migrants and to ensure the full implementation of these rights.

Notes

1/ According to the World Labour Report (Geneva, International Labour Office, 1984), the stock of economically active migrants in 1980, was between 19.7 and 21.7 million.

2/ "Welfare of migrant workers and their families: progress report of the Secretary-General" (E/CN.5/568).

3/ A. Lebon and C. Falchi, "New developments in intra-European migration since 1974", International Migration Review, vol. XIV, No. 4 (1980), p. 545.

4/ W. R. Böhning, "International migration in Western Europe: reflections of the past five years", International Labour Review, vol. 118, No. 4 (1979).

5/ Organisation for Economic Co-operation and Development. SOPEMI (Continuous reporting system on migration) (Paris, 1982), p. 33.

6/ Council of Europe, "Report on the situation of migrant workers and members of their families: Achievements, problems and possible solutions", Second Conference of European Ministers Responsible for Migration Affairs, Strasbourg, 1983, p. 3.

7/ Organisation for Economic Co-operation and Development, "Working Party on the Role of Women in the Economy: women and their integration in the economy – note by the secretariat" (Paris, 1984), p. 115 (MAS/WP6(84)5).

8/ World Labour Report (Geneva, International Labour Office, 1984), p. 107.

9/ Lionel Demery, "Asian labour migration to the Middle East: an empirical assessment", paper presented to the Conference on Asian Labour Migration to the Middle East, Honolulu, Hawaii, 19–23 September 1983.

10/ "Welfare of migrant workers ...", p. 5, para. 13.

11/ John E. Smart and Virginia A. Teodosio, "Skills and earnings: issues in the developmental impact of Middle East employment on the Philippines", paper presented to the Conference on Asian Labour Migration to the Middle East, Honolulu, Hawaii, 19–23 September 1983.

12/ Nasra M. Shah, "Pakistani workers in the Middle East: volume, trends and consequences", International Migration Review, vol. XVII, No. 3 (1983), pp. 410–424.

13/ Vichitra Prompunthum, "Policies and programs concerning labour migration from Thailand to the Middle East", paper presented to the Conference on Asian Labour Migration to the Middle East, Honolulu, Hawaii, 19–23 September 1983.

14/ Smart and Teodosio, op. cit.

15/ Ijaz Gilani, "Overview of stocks and flows of migrants and the social and familial impacts on communities and households in districts of high labour migration", paper presented to the Conference on Asian Labour Migration to the Middle East, Honolulu, Hawaii, 19–23 September 1983.

16/ World Labour Report ..., p. 108.

17/ Ibid., p. 101.

18/ International Migration Policies and Programmes: A World Survey (United Nations publication, Sales No. E.82.XIII.4).

19/ Donald Kalinde Kowet, "Social situation of migrant workers and their families in Africa", paper prepared for the United Nations (1984), p. 4.

20/ K. C. Zachariah and Julien Condé, "Migration in West Africa, demographic aspects", a joint World Bank-OECD study (New York, Oxford University Press, 1981), p. 39.

21/ Charles W. Stahl, "Singapore's foreign workforce: some reflections on its benefits and costs", International Migration Review, vol. XVIII, No. 1 (1984), pp. 37–49.

22/ Charles W. Stahl, "Labour migration amongst the ASEAN countries" (New South Wales, University of Newcastle, 1983).

23/ According to a recent report of the Council of Europe, the average duration of residence in the Federal Republic of Germany is 9.5 years; in France 70 per cent of the foreigners have been resident for more than 11 years, and in Switzerland 80 per cent have been resident for 6 years or more.

24/ Eric-Jean Thomas, Immigrant Workers in Europe: Their Legal Status - A Comparative Study (Paris, United Nations Educational, Scientific and Cultural Organization, 1982).

25/ "Migrant workers: Pertinent legislative and administrative regulations on the welfare of migrant workers and their families" (ST/ESA/132).

26/ W. R. Böhning, "International migration: implications for development and policies", paper presented to the International Conference on Population, 1984, Expert Group Meeting on Population Distribution, Migration and Development, Hamamet, Tunisia, 21-25 March 1983, p. 5.

27/ Elisabeth Gordon, "Analysis of the impact of labour-migration on the lives of women in Lesotho", Journal of Development Studies, vol. 17, No. 3 (April 1981), p. 73.

28/ Bager Al-Najjar, "Work and living conditions of foreign workers", Foreign Labour in the Arab Gulf Countries, 1982, p. 99.

29/ Ministry of Planning, Annual Statistical Abstract, 1981 (Kuwait), p. 51.

30/ Al Watan (Kuwait), 18 April 1984, p. 1.

31/ Migrant Workers, General Survey by the Committee of Experts on the Application of Conventions and Recommendations, International Labour Conference, 66th session, 1980 (Geneva, International Labour Office, 1981).

32/ "Pertinent regulations concerning the welfare of migrant workers and their families: report of the Secretary-General" (E/CN.5/1983/10), p. 23.

33/ Yves Charbit, "Children of migrant workers and their home countries", paper presented to the International Symposium, Ankara, 7-10 June 1977, p. 28.

34/ Institute of Labour and Manpower Studies, "Socio-economic consequences of contract labour migration in the Philippines", Technical report (Manila, Ministry of Labour and Employment, 1983), vol. 11, p. 60.

35/ Peerathep Roongshivin, "Some socio-economic consequences of Thailand's migration to the Middle East", paper presented to the Conference on Asian Labour Migration to the Middle East, Honolulu, Hawaii, 19-23 September 1983.

36/ Charles W. Stahl, "International labour migration and the ASEAN economies", International Migration for Employment Working Paper No. 13 (Geneva, International Labour Office, 1984).

37/ Council of Europe, Draft Report on Migrant Women (Strasbourg, 1982), p. 8 (AS/PR(33)21).

38/ Charbit, op. cit., p. 85.

39/ "The welfare of migrant workers and their families" (SOA/ESDP/1975/3), p. 72.

40/ R.B.M. Korale, "Migration for employment to the Middle East: its demographic and socio-economic effects on Sri Lanka", paper presented to the Conference on Asian Labour Migration to the Middle East, Honolulu, Hawaii, 19-23 September 1983.

41/ Leela Gulati, "Impacts of male migration to the Middle East on the family: some evidence from Kerala", paper presented to the Conference on Asian Labour Migration to the Middle East, Honolulu, Hawaii, 19-23 September 1983.

42/ Kyong-Dong Kim and On-Jook Lee, "Social-psychological implications of international labour migration: the case of Korean workers in the Middle East and their families", paper presented to the Conference on Asian Labour Migration to the Middle East, Honolulu, Hawaii, 19-23 September 1983.

43/ Stella P. Go, Leticia T. Postrado and Pilar Ramos-Jimenez, "The effects of international contract labour" (Manila, Integrated Research Center, De La Salle University, 1983), vol. I.

44/ Gilani, op. cit.

45/ Fred Arnold and Nasra M. Shah, "Asian labor migration to the Middle-East", International Migration Review, vol. XVIII, No. 2 (1984), p. 306.

46/ Fred Arnold, "The social situation of Asian migrant workers and their families" (Honolulu, Hawaii, East-West Population Institute).

47/ W. A. Dumon, "Family migration and family reunion", ICEM Second Seminar on Adaptation and Integration of Permanent Immigrants (Geneva, Intergovernmental Committee for European Migration, 1975), vol. XIV, p. 70.

48/ "Pertinent regulations concerning the welfare of migrant workers and their families: report of the Secretary-General" (E/CN.5/1983/10), pp. 12-17.

49/ Herbert Leuminger, "The migrant family: socio-political problems and responsibilities", Migration News (Geneva, International Catholic Migration Commission, 1981).

50/ Migrants' Children and Employment: The European Experience (Paris, Organisation for Economic Co-operation and Development, 1983), p. 7.

51/ "The welfare of migrant workers and their families" (SOA/ESDP/1975/3), p. 80.

52/ Jonas Widgren, The Position of Second-Generation Migrants in Europe. UNDP/ILO European regional project for second-generation migrants. (Geneva, International Labour Office, 1982).

53/ Peter Fendrich, SOPEMI Report on the Federal Republic of Germany, (Paris, Organisation for Economic Co-operation and Development, 1980), p. 31.

54/ Koula Kassimati, "Recent studies and research on return migration: lessons to be drawn for policies on vocational, social and cultural (re)integration of second-generation migrants if they return", paper prepared for the UNDP/ILO European Regional Project for Second-Generation Migrants (Geneva, International Labour Office, 1982).

55/ Milenia Cvetic, "Vocational pre-training and training of second generation migrants", paper prepared for the UNDP/ILO European Regional Project for Second-Generation Migrants (Geneva, International Labour Office, 1982), p. 12.

56/ Widgren, op. cit., p. 21.

57/ Leslie J. Limaga, "The situation of young women migrants of the second-generation in Western Europe", paper prepared for the UNDP/ILO European Regional Project for Second-Generation Migrants (Geneva, International Labour Office, 1981).

58/ Widgren, op. cit., p. 22.

59/ Limaga, op. cit., p. 10.

60/ International Migration Review, vol. XV, No. 4, p. 695.

61/ Migrants' Children and Employment. The European Experience (Paris, Organisation for Economic Co-operation and Development, 1983).

62/ Council of Europe, "Report on the situation of migrant workers ...", p. 23.

63/ Organisation for Economic Co-operation and Development, "Working Party on the Role of Women in the Economy: women and their integration in the economy - note by the secretariat" (Paris, 1984), p. 134 (MAS/WP6(84)5).

64/ Ibid., p. 135.

65/ Bassem Sirhan, "Social condition of migrant workers in the major labour receiving ECWA countries", paper prepared for the United Nations (1984), p. 7.

66/ Arab Planning Institute, Information File of Foreign Labour in the Gulf (Kuwait, 1982), p. 22.

67/ Bassem, op. cit., p. 22.

68/ Coulibali Sidiki, Gregory Joel, Piché Victor, "L'immigration étrangère dans le Plan de développement economique, social et culturel 1976-80 de la République du Côte d'Ivoire", Seminaire de sensibilisation aux problèmes de migrations en Haute-Volta, 3-9 mars 1980 (Ouagadougou, 1980), pp. 134-142 (DRD/INSD).

69/ Council of Europe, Committee on Migration, Refugees and Demography, Draft Report on Manifestations of Xenophobia in the Member States towards Migrant Workers (Strasbourg, 1983) (AS/PR(35)9).

70/ The Economist, 17-23 September 1983.

71/ Council of Europe, Draft Report on Manifestations ..., pp. 8-10.

72/ "1982 report of the Federal Republic of Germany in continuous reporting system on migration (SOPEMI)" (Paris, Organisation for Economic Co-operation and Development, 1982), pp. 31-32.

73/ Ivo Baucic, "Report on employment situation of second-generation migrants in Europe", prepared for the ILO Tripartite Technical Seminar on Second Generation Migrants, Lisbon, 4-9 May 1981 (Geneva, International Labour Office, 1981), p. 24.

74/ Council of Europe, Report on the Return of Migrant Workers to their Country of Origin (Strasbourg, 1985), p. 8 (doc. 5379).

- 63 -

75/ Baucic, op. cit., pp. 27-29.

76/ Josip Anic and others, "The development of economic migration from the countries of south Europe and the Mediterranean and its social consequences", p. 22.

77/ Gilani, op. cit.

78/ International Migration Policies and Programmes: ..., p. 108.

79/ World Labour Report ..., p. 112.

80/ See, for example, Judith Miller, "Foreign workers live hard life in Saudi Arabia", New York Times, 15 October 1983.